THE REAL READER'S QU....

Slightly Foxed

'Voices from the Riverbank'

NO.74   SUMMER 2022

Editors: Gail Pirkis & Hazel Wood
Editorial & submissions: Anna Kirk
Marketing & publicity: Steph Allen, Jennie Harrison Bunning & Hattie Summers
Subscriptions, orders & bookshops: Jess Dalby

Cover illustration: Clover Robin, 'Devon Coastal Path, 2022'

Clover Robin is a collage artist and the illustrator of several books for children. Her cover image was inspired by the stunning South-West Coast Path that she has walked since childhood. She has recently returned to Devon after thirteen years of living in London. Nature and the outdoors are recurring themes in her work and continue to inspire the spontaneous and evocative landscapes she loves to create. For more of her work visit www.cloverrobin.com or follow her on Instagram @clover_robin

Design by Octavius Murray
Layout by Andrew Evans
Colophon and tailpiece by David Eccles

Published by Slightly Foxed Limited
53 Hoxton Square
London N1 6PB

tel 020 7033 0258
email office@foxedquarterly.com
www.foxedquarterly.com

Slightly Foxed is published quarterly in early March, June, September and December

Annual subscription rates (4 issues)
UK and Ireland £48; Overseas £56

Single copies of this issue can be bought for £12.50 (UK) or £14.50 (Overseas)

All back issues in printed form are also available

ISBN 978-1-910898-68-0
ISSN 1742-5794

Printed and bound by Smith Settle, Yeadon, West Yorkshire

Contents

Contents

Clare Curtis

The Slightly Foxed Podcast

A new episode of our podcast is available on the 15th of April, July, October and January. To listen, visit www.foxedquarterly.com/pod or search for Slightly Foxed on Audioboom, Apple Podcasts or your podcast app.

Subscriber Benefits

Slightly Foxed can obtain any books reviewed in this issue, whether new or second-hand. To enquire about a book, to access the digital edition of *Slightly Foxed* or to view a list of membership benefits, visit www.foxedquarterly.com/members or contact the office: 020 7033 0258/office@foxedquarterly.com.

From the Editors

Summer is here and the square outside has come alive again. There are people walking their dogs or enjoying the sunshine at tables outside the café opposite the office. It's a peaceful scene, but it's impossible to forget that far away though ever-present is this year's ugly backdrop of the war in Ukraine, not to mention the violence and suppression of free speech in so many parts of the world. We've never taken ourselves too seriously at *Slightly Foxed*, seeing it as essentially a place where readers can relax, enjoy good writing and, we hope, have a laugh occasionally. But in these deeply worrying and isolating times, it's the comforting sense of fellowship and connection through books that readers tell us they get from *Slightly Foxed* which seems especially important.

It does, at any rate, look as if foreign travel will be possible again this summer, and this issue features a number of good travel reads to pack into the suitcase, from Eric Newby's wry and funny account of his attempt on an unclimbed peak in the Hindu Kush to the exploits of the colourful characters who ventured on secret missions into High Asia in the days of Empire, described by Peter Hopkirk in *The Great Game*.

In the spring we reissued *Lark Rise*, the first volume in Flora Thompson's lightly fictionalized account of growing up in the last decades of the nineteenth century in the then remote Oxfordshire hamlet of Juniper Hill. Our new Slightly Foxed Edition continues Flora's story through the two final books in the trilogy, *Over to Candleford* and *Candleford Green* (see p.13). They are, if possible, even more enjoyable than the first, for in them life broadens out for Flora

– or Laura as she calls her younger self – when she pays her first visit to her father's relatives in Candleford, the local market town, and makes particular friends with her uncle Tom, who like her is a reader and one of life's observers. Flora's education continues when she finds a job as assistant to the postmistress in a nearby village: *Candleford Green* is an enchanting picture of a young and sensitive girl growing up in this small but colourful community, and of Dorcas Lane, Flora's redoubtable – and unforgettable – new employer.

When titles in our limited and numbered Slightly Foxed Editions sell out, we've been gradually making the most popular ones available again as Plain Foxed Editions – the same attractive and readable hardback format, but without the frills. This summer's PFE is a treat, *Another Self* by James Lees-Milne, one of the linchpins of the early National Trust, and keeper of one of the best and most amusing diaries ever written. In this memoir he looks back with disarming candour, and perhaps a little imaginative embroidery, to the follies and misjudgements of his awkward younger self in the upper-class milieu in which he grew up. It's perfect light holiday reading, charming and very funny.

GAIL PIRKIS & HAZEL WOOD

Voices from the Riverbank

SUE GEE

'Never read it?' said the Rat in astonishment. 'Never *read* it? Why, my dear fellow, you simply haven't lived.'

'Is it really as good as all that?' the Mole asked humbly.

The Rat pulled up a fireside chair. 'Sit down, and let me explain.'

This little passage comes not from *The Wind in the Willows* (1908) but from my own pen, written in homage, and the Rat's sentiments echo mine entirely. I have loved and revisited Kenneth Grahame's masterpiece since I was 8 when, in a school test, I read aloud the scene in which Toad, imprisoned for stealing a motor car, is brought hot buttered toast by the gaoler's daughter. What bliss.

To this day, I often sort the laundry murmuring the words spoken by a passing fox to the furious Toad who, disguised as a washerwoman in order to escape from prison, is forced to keep up the deception by actually doing the work. 'Half a pair of socks and a pillowcase missing this week,' remarks the fox. 'Mind it doesn't occur again.'

Kenneth Grahame, *The Wind in the Willows* (1908), illus. E. H. Shepard · Farshore · Hb · 224pp · £12.99 · ISBN 9781405297820; Peter Hunt, *The Making of The Wind in the Willows* (2018) · Bodleian Library · Pb · 128pp · £12.99 · ISBN 9781851244799; Matthew Dennison, *Eternal Boy: The Life of Kenneth Grahame* (2018) · Head of Zeus · Pb · 304pp · £8.99 · ISBN 9781786697745

As for 'More speeches by Toad', the line which appears several times in the programme Toad himself devises to celebrate his triumphant return: on how many occasions do these words come to mind as someone, quite possibly a man, Goes On?

Last year my bibliophile sister-in-law gave me for Christmas the one hundred and second edition (1951), with glorious colour plates by Arthur Rackham. It is this edition I have returned to now, with an introduction by A. A. Milne, whose theatre box was shared by Kenneth Grahame and his wife in December 1929, to the delight of all parties, on the opening night of *Toad of Toad Hall.*

'When characters have been created as solidly as those of Rat, Mole, Toad and Badger, they speak ever after in their own voices,' writes Milne, 'and the dramatist has merely to listen and record.'

The kindly, river-loving Rat, 'a poet of independent means' as one critic has it, the cautious and endearing Mole, the impossibly arrogant Toad and reclusive, fatherly Badger: where did they come from, these beloved creatures, and what do we know of the man who created them?

Kenneth Grahame was born in Edinburgh in 1859, the eldest of four children. Their mother was connected by birth to the Duke of Argyll; their advocate father had been appointed sheriff to the county. Family life came to an end when their mother died of scarlet fever, and her husband sank into drink.

At the age of 5 Kenneth was sent with his siblings to stay with their maternal grandmother at The Mount, an old, patched-up house in Cookham Dean, Berkshire, whose gardens ran down to the Thames. As Matthew Dennison, Grahame's most recent biographer, describes it, the atmosphere created by their grandmother was frosty, but the house itself, and the neighbouring fields, woods and peaceful stretch of river became places of enchantment.

Dennison sees Grahame as a man who never recovered from his early bereavement and remained in thrall to his childhood. Peter Hunt, author of *The Making of The Wind in the Willows* (2018),

presents quite a different picture: of a 'remarkable and surprising man', successful, clubbable, at ease. It is an indication of Grahame's complexity that he should inspire such different views; the fact remains that he was someone who, no matter how much of a lonely, bereaved little boy he was deep down, dealt manfully with disappointment and made the best of things.

The first disappointment came when his uncle refused to send him to Oxford. He was very bright; he longed to go; there was no money. Instead, he left St Edward's School, Oxford, where he had begun to love the city, and sat the entrance exam for a gentleman clerk at the Bank of England, scoring 100 per cent. He arrived at the Bank at the age of 19 and never left, rising to become Secretary and an unequivocally Establishment figure.

But there was much about Grahame that was absolutely not Establishment. Feeling himself a writer from an early age, by the 1890s he was writing short stories for periodicals such as the *National Observer*, gravitating from there to the more outré *Yellow Book*, a quarterly associated with Aubrey Beardsley, its first art editor, and Oscar Wilde. At this point, alongside his sober life at the Bank, Grahame was very much the carefree bachelor about literary London. In 1895 his first collection of stories, for adults but featuring a group of children, *The Golden Age*, was published, followed by *Dream Days* (1898), which returned to the same childhood world. Both were extremely popular.

Charming, good-looking – his agent Curtis Brown described him as 'the handsomest man I ever saw' – and an established author, in 1897 he was introduced to a woman with her own literary ambitions: Elspeth Thomson, an heiress admired by Tenniel, unmarried and largely unpublished. She was determined to capture him; Grahame, who had so far avoided all romantic attachments, succumbed. They were married in 1899, he aged 40, she not much younger. Both were virgins.

Alastair, their only child, always known as Mouse, was born ten months later, the product of what seems to have otherwise been an almost sexless marriage. Certainly Elspeth was soon writing to her friend Florence Hardy of her disappointment in that regard (something poor Florence understood only too well). It has been conjectured that Grahame was essentially homosexual, but if so it never found expression, unless you choose to read *The Wind in the Willows* as code. Certainly for much of the marriage he was living and working in London, and Elspeth was in the country, but they also spent time together travelling, leaving Mouse, a half-blind but spirited little boy, in the charge of a governess.

It was on a trip to Cornwall that Grahame wrote to his son, then aged 7, an affectionate letter which recounted Toad's theft of a motor car from 'The Red Lion Hotel' in 'a town called Bugglestone'. A later letter tells of Toad's encounter with the bargee who realizes he is not a washerwoman at all, and hurls him into the canal – 'Splosh!!'

It was all there in embryo, and it developed when in 1908 Grahame left London and retired with his wife and child to Cookham Dean, the gentle English village which had so captivated him as a little boy. Here, the letters became bedtime stories, and the stories found their setting in the places of his childhood: the riverbank, and the woods that became the Wild Wood, where Ratty and Mole get lost on a snowy winter's night. Here, within six months, Kenneth Grahame wrote the book of his life.

With more time to write than he had enjoyed for years, perhaps he was recapturing his carefree bachelor days, and gently satirizing a few old friends. 'For animals read chaps,' as the critic Margaret Blount has written. He drew on Hilaire Belloc, whose Thameside house probably inspired Toad Hall; on Arthur Quiller-Couch, with whom he went sailing in Cornwall. The bewhiskered W. E. Henley, his first publisher, was a possible model for Toad. He had, you sense, enormous enjoyment in the writing.

And appealing to both children and adults, *The Wind in the Willows* is as near perfect as any book could be. It's immensely energetic and it has a huge emotional range. The prose is immaculate, the dialogue sings. The structure is that of a classic epic, contrasting wild adventure with cherished home, whose last chapter is entitled 'The Return of Ulysses'. The authorial voice, often very funny, speaks with immense affection of every aspect of the natural world – 'hedgerows . . . copses . . . everywhere birds building, flowers budding, leaves thrusting, everything happy, and progressive, and occupied', as Mole finds it when he flings down his whitewash brush and sets out across country one fine spring morning.

This is the book's first adventure; many are to come, including car crashes, the famous escape from prison and the most fantastic train ride; the terror of the Wild Wood and the violent – really violent – recapturing of Toad Hall.

Set against all this activity is a great deal of domestic life (and a very great deal of good food). Whether Rat's 'bijou riverside residence', shabby but beloved Mole End, Badger's rambling underground retreat or the magnificent Toad Hall, each of these homes is so described as to make the reader long to step inside – to live there, even.

The Wind in the Willows is loved, now, all over the world. Italians read it as *Il Vento nei Salici*; in Afrikaans it becomes *Die Wind in die Wilgers*. Grahame's own working title was *Mole and His Mates*. At

Methuen, where Curtis Brown finally placed the book – other publishers had turned it down as too eccentric a departure from Grahame's well-loved stories of the past – it went through various incarnations, including *The Wind in the Reeds*. We shall never know which inspired employee hit upon the alliteration which makes that title now as much a part of English literature as *Hamlet* or *The Secret Garden*.

What is the book really about? Grahame is so very good on happiness and contentment, and a large part of its popularity is surely due to the fact that it makes you happy. But although he wrote it before the tragedy of Mouse's suicide at the age of 19, he also understands sorrow, and loss, and above all the deep meaning of home and belonging. Yes, it is a profoundly conservative book, whose values were overturned in Jan Needle's *Wild Wood* (1982), retelling the whole story from the viewpoint of what Grahame would have regarded as the lower orders. But in the descriptions of Mole's sudden longing for Mole End, and Toad's despair at the loss of Toad Hall, Grahame shows himself acutely aware of what it means to lose your whole identity, to be cast adrift.

For all its jollity, escapades and fun, *The Wind in the Willows* is essentially about loss and recovery. Perhaps, above all, Grahame was writing not just to Mouse but to himself as a child, creating the kind of book he would like to have read then, while drawing on all parts of himself as a man.

SUE GEE's book of essays, *Just You and the Page: Twelve Writers and Their Art*, is published by Seren Books (2021). You can also hear her discuss the art of editing on our podcast, Episode 3, 'Stet'. The illustrations in this article are by Ernest H. Shepard.

An Understanding Heart

HAZEL WOOD

I can't remember when I first read the magical trilogy that came to be known as *Lark Rise to Candleford* but, turning to it for comfort during the days of the 2020 lockdowns, I was struck afresh by the wonderful clarity and assurance of the writing. Most memoirs at the time Flora Thompson was writing were by comfortably educated, middle-class people, while she grew up as the daughter of a poor bricklayer in a small Oxfordshire village. Yet from the first sentence you feel the authenticity of her voice and know you are in the hands of an accomplished writer. As her biographer Margaret Lane put it, 'She was able to write the annals of the poor because she was one of them.'

The first volume in the trilogy, *Lark Rise* (SFE no. 58), recreates in lightly fictionalized form Flora's childhood in the Oxfordshire hamlet of Juniper Hill (Lark Rise of the title) during the last years of the nineteenth century. It is an extraordinary feat of memory, for it was written almost fifty years after the events it describes. The hamlet is recalled in minute and exquisite detail, a close-up, child's-eye view of a small, self-sufficient world bounded by cornfields and peopled by familiar characters.

In its sequel, *Over to Candleford*, life begins to open out for Flora – or Laura as she calls her childhood self – as she leaves Lark Rise on a visit to her father's relations in Candleford, the local market town. For the children it's a long-anticipated adventure.

Very early one Sunday morning, while the rest of the hamlet was still asleep and the sky was still pink and the garden flowers and currant bushes were still greyish-rough with dew, they

13

heard the sound of wheels drawing up at their gate and knew that the innkeeper's old pony had come with the spring cart to take them.

In Candleford Flora is introduced to the households of her two uncles – James, a prosperous builder and pillar of the Temperance movement, and Tom, a liberal thinker and respected craftsman whose workshop produces ladies' made-to-measure shoes and hunting boots.

Both have done well for themselves, but there the likeness ends, for in the first family Flora feels overwhelmed by the grand house and rich food, and patronized by her more sophisticated – not to say pretentious – cousins, while in the second all is generosity, warmth and welcome, and over time and successive visits she forms a special bond with her Uncle Tom, for they both love reading and he introduces her to books and to unusual people – known to the family as Tom's 'queer fish' – whom she would never have met in Lark Rise.

The close of this second book finds teenage Laura at home once more, unhappy and undecided about her future. Fortunately the decision is made for her by a letter from an old friend of her mother's, who runs the Post Office in a village a few miles from Candleford and is looking for an assistant. This is the setting for *Candleford Green*, an enchanting portrait of a village community and of Dorcas Lane, Laura's redoubtable new employer, with her well-ordered household, high standards and firm traditional views. 'She's a clever one, that Miss Lane, as sharp as vinegar but not bad in her way,' people in the village would say to Laura.

Miss Lane is certainly in control of her small empire, including the village smithy next door to the Post Office, a family business which, unusually for a woman, she has inherited and continues to run. She keeps a close but discreet eye on village life from her vantage point on the village green, and is on excellent terms with such local notables as Sir Timothy, the local landowner and Justice of the Peace, a benign figure who gives off an aura of 'jollity, good sense and good nature, together with the smell of tobacco, stables and country tweeds', when he swears Laura in to her new employment On Her Majesty's Service. And when, twice a year, Mr Rushton, the head postmaster from Candleford, appears on what is supposed to be a surprise visit, he always personally phones ahead to tell Miss Lane he is coming. This saves trouble all round and leaves plenty of time for sociability and a generous tea.

For Laura, life with Miss Lane introduces her to a world of plentiful food and comfortable living that she has never experienced before. Eating and sleeping under Miss Lane's roof, in addition to Laura, are old Zillah the somewhat grumpy maid, three shy but friendly young apprentice blacksmiths and their foreman Matthew, a small, bent, elderly man who keeps a tame thrush whose wing he has mended, and who is more at ease with animals than people. This is a kind of liberation for Laura. For the first time she is the youngest person in a household of adults, whereas at home she had been a little mother to her younger brothers and sisters. 'Her thin figure filled out, a brighter colour appeared in her cheeks, and such an inrush of energy and high spirits took hold of her that she would dance, rather than walk, about the house and garden, and felt she could never tire.'

Sue Scullard

When for the first time she is entrusted with the job of

delivering the post to the great house on an icy winter morning the freedom she feels is intoxicating.

> Laura never forgot that morning's walk. Fifty years later she could recall it in detail. Snow had fallen a few days earlier, then had frozen, and on the hard crust yet more snow had fallen and lay like soft, feathery down, fleecing the surface of the level open spaces of the park and softening the outlines of hillocks and fences. Against it the dark branches and twigs of the trees stood out lacelike. The sky was low and grey and soft-looking as a feather-bed.

This new life is Laura's first real step out into the world, and an ideal situation for a budding writer, for the whole colourful society of Candleford Green passes daily through the Post Office. Flora's ability to catch the telling detail brings them vividly alive: Old Mr Stokes, the church organist and cabinet-maker who had actually built the church organ and still worked at his trade 'with his long lean form swathed in a white apron and his long white beard tucked into his waistcoat'; mysterious Mrs Macey the postwoman, who 'instead of plodding or sauntering country fashion, walked firmly and quickly, as if with a destination in view'. And Flora saw into the hearts of those around her, observing of Mrs Macey that though some villagers called her sour-looking, 'anyone with more penetration would have known that she was not sour but sad'.

Yet despite the excitement of these new experiences, including a brief meeting with a sympathetic, bookish young reporter for the *Candleford News*, which gives her a glimpse of what it is to share a real interest with someone of her own age, there is always a part of Flora that yearns for the countryside of her childhood and the simple warmth of the family she has left behind. Some of her most poignant and evocative writing describes her joy at coming home for a weekend, walking through the fields from Candleford, then the mixed emotions of saying goodbye to her mother early on a Monday morning.

> Her mother put on her thick cape and walked to the turn of the hamlet road with her. It was a raw grey winter morning with stars paling in a veil of cottage chimney smoke . . . although not frosty, the air was cold and the two snuggled closely together, Laura's arm in her mother's under the cape. She had grown so much that she had to lean down to her mother, and they laughed at that and recalled the time when she, a tiny mite, had said: 'Some day, when I'm grown up, I'll be the mother and you'll be my little girl.' At the turn of the road they halted and, after a close embrace, her mother said goodbye in the old country words: 'Goodbye. God bless you!'

Flora wrote these two final books of the trilogy in the dark days of the Second World War, and perhaps it was partly this that made her happy memories of this period in her life shine so brightly. Soon Candleford Green would become a mere suburb and the old self-sufficient life of the hamlet would disappear, but for us they are still there as they were during those last decades of the nineteenth century, captured for ever by Flora's understanding heart and the beautiful economy of her writing.

HAZEL WOOD is a city-dweller who, like Flora Thompson, feels the pull of the countryside in which she grew up.

Flora Thompson's *Over to Candleford* (1941) and *Candleford Green* (1943) are now available in a single 400-page volume, in a limited and numbered cloth-bound edition of 2,000 copies (subscribers: UK & Eire £18, Overseas £20; non-subscribers: UK & Eire £20, Overseas £22). All prices include post and packing. Copies may be ordered by post (53 Hoxton Square, London N1 6PB), by phone (020 7033 0258) or via our website www.foxedquarterly.com.

In Nuristan with Carless

JUSTIN MAROZZI

Twenty years ago, I was due to give a talk at the Travellers Club about a recent expedition. I thought it would be much more entertaining for everyone if my friend Ned spoke about the perils of travelling with a travel writer. Eventually we also invited the retired diplomat Hugh Carless, a fellow victim, to talk about his own dire experiences at the hands of Eric Newby in *A Short Walk in the Hindu Kush* (1958). By then in his late seventies, Carless was charming, extremely modest and very funny. Rather unkindly, I thought, someone asked if his Foreign Office career had ever recovered from his merciless treatment. He laughed uncomfortably.

Newby died a few years later, followed in 2012 by Carless. Today my copy of *A Short Walk* sits on my desk, its cover and spine as crumpled and weather-beaten as its late author in his octogenarian dotage. Inside the cover it is inscribed in faded biro:

Silvio Marozzi
Tripoli
Socialist People's Libyan Arab Jamahiriya
1st March 1986

I don't know why my father used the full, bombastic name for Gaddafi's Libya (I suspect it was out of caution while working in this

---

Eric Newby, *A Short Walk in the Hindu Kush* (1958)
Collins · Pb · 256pp · £9.99 · ISBN 9780007367757
Eric Newby's *Something Wholesale* (1962) and *Love and War in the Apennines* (1971) are both available as Slightly Foxed Editions.

unpredictable dictatorship), but I do know that Eric Newby's comic masterpiece was one of his favourite and best-loved books, a master-class in travel writing. He must have passed this Picador edition on to me shortly afterwards because I can't remember a time when I didn't have it. And every time I look at it, it reminds me I should have been much more ruthless about Ned, who got off very lightly when compared with Carless.

First published in 1958, *A Short Walk in the Hindu Kush* has long since acquired mythic status. Hundreds of thousands of paperbacks have been sold around the world, and readers continue to be charmed by its big-hearted embrace of overseas adventure, its hapless amateur-ishness, its quintessentially British self-deprecation (is there another nation on earth that boasts so relentlessly about its modesty?) and its delicious humour.

Two bored Brits, without a shred of mountaineering experience between them, decide on a whim to attempt an unclimbed 19,000-foot peak in the Hindu Kush mountains of Afghanistan. What could possibly go wrong? Its celebrated ending, which we shall come to later, has taken its place on the same pedestal of remote literary encounters as Henry Morton Stanley's 'Dr Livingstone, I presume?'

Let's deal with the humour first and state from the outset that this is a very funny book. Many of us may wince at the expression 'laugh-out-loud', but during my latest rereading of the book in bed, I immediately began to annoy my wife (not an uncommon situation) by bursting into laughter every few minutes. The best way to counter her irritation, it seemed to me, was to read out the particular passage. For once I was right, and we were both in hysterics.

The same is true, incidentally, of Newby's outrageously funny memoir, *Something Wholesale*, an account of his decade-long dalli-ance with the rag trade. The end of that career in couture, an unlikely postscript for a man who had fought with distinction in the Special Boat Service during the war, was the springboard for his 'short walk'. 'CAN YOU TRAVEL NURISTAN JUNE?' Newby telegrammed Carless in

Rio de Janeiro. With a three-word reply – 'OF COURSE HUGH' – the adventure was on.

If the book's title is a sit-up-and-take-notice pointer to the richly self-effacing Newby style (to call this brutal expedition a short walk is to test understatement to breaking point), the chapter headings follow the same direction. Chapter 1 is 'Life of a Salesman', swiftly juxtaposed with Chapter 2's 'Death of a Salesman' and the irrepressible, phoenix-like Chapter 3: 'Birth of a Mountain Climber'.

Newby discovers with horror the true extent of Carless's mountaineering ambitions in an increasingly voluminous correspondence recommending the purchase of large quantities of specialist equipment. Newbie Newby has second thoughts.

I told Wanda my wife.

'I think he's insane,' she said, 'just dotty. What will happen if you say no?'

'I already have but he doesn't take any notice.'

After a four-day crash course in mountaineering in Wales, where they learn the rudimentary arts of ropework and belaying, it's off to Turkey for the overland journey to Afghanistan, Wanda in tow for the initial leg.

At this point a word or two about Carless is in order. He has the distinction in these pages, unfortunate for him but gloriously entertaining for readers, of serving that essential literary role: the Travel Writer's Foil. With a few strokes of Newby's pen he becomes the right-thinking, inflexible, impatient, occasionally stern British official, forever saying things like 'We must leave at once.' The straight-man set pieces are brilliantly done, the joshing remorseless. Newby is never careless with Carless.

After a navigating blunder which leaves them undiplomatically close to the Russian border with a car full of cameras, telescopes, compasses and maps, Carless is determined to turn around.

We argued with him in the growing darkness, even made fun of him, but it was of no use, he was beyond the reach of humour. On his face was a look that I had never seen. He spoke with an air of absolute certainty, like a man under the influence of drugs. Like the Mole in *The Wind in the Willows* picking up the scent of his old home, Hugh was in direct contact with the Foreign Office, SW1, and the scent was breast-high.

Arriving at last in Kabul, they discover the government has assigned them a guide for their assault on the elusive peak of Mir Samir. The Afghan's qualifications appear dubious. He has just returned from riding around the world on a bicycle.

Against my will I found myself conducting a sort of viva voce examination of this formidable being.

'Have you had any previous climbing experience?'

'None at all,' he said, and my heart warmed to him. 'But I did run in the ten thousand metres in the Asian Games,' he added modestly.

Travelling through Tajik country up the Panjshir valley with Abdul Ghiyas, a more suitable guide, they make camp at 8,000 feet one night and Carless regales, at considerable length, a local mullah and various horse drivers with his previous adventures.

Hugh was telling an interminable story, something from South America, about an anaconda killing a horse. To express it in classical Persian was heavy going; judging by the look of almost hysterical concentration on the faces of his audience it was pretty difficult for them too.

Inevitably the British travellers' health deteriorates. Frazzled with heat, racked with thirst and drop-dead exhausted, they down draughts of local water. Then Carless, who perversely considers himself immune to water-borne disease, reluctantly admits to being unwell.

'Diarrhoea. It's most unusual.'
  'I'm not a bit surprised. It's all this filthy water we're drinking.'
  'There's nothing wrong with the water.'
  'Perhaps we're not strong enough for it.'
  'You have to get used to it.'
  'Like old women drinking meths?'

It is a tragedy that, thanks to the series of wars that have raged more or less continuously in Afghanistan since the ill-fated Soviet invasion of 1979, many in the West today equate the country with the Taliban, Al Qaeda and terrorism. That is like judging the UK exclusively through the prism of its relationship with the EU. It is worth emphasizing the sheer heart-stopping beauty of the country and the humbling hospitality of its people, which completely captivate travellers. Newby was no exception and, comic precision aside, his prose sings with a finely tuned sense of place.

Up and up the Panjshir they slog until, one evening, turning a corner in the road, 'suddenly we were in paradise . . . poplars shimmered; willows bowed in the breeze; water flowed slowly in the irrigation ditches through a hundred gardens, among apricot trees with the fruit still heavy on them, submerging the butts of the mulberries, whose owners squatted in their properties and viewed the scene with satisfaction'. It was like 'some golden age of human happiness' which communicated its magic to all who were there. Not for nothing is this wild eastern region known as Nuristan, Land of Light.

Snatches of history, geography and nature writing maintain the narrative thrust, but laconic humour is the thread that binds it all together. One morning they spy a vast, snow-covered peak at the top of the Darra Ghuzu valley. An old man sitting by the road asks where they are going.

'*Kuh-i-Mir Samir*. We are going to climb it.'
  'Ghuzu', he said, pointing to the impressive pinnacle, 'is

nothing but a child. *Kuh-i-Mir Samir* is a great mountain. It is quite vertical. No man can reach the summit.'

For some time we plodded on in silence while I digested this unpalatable information.

Without giving the game away, the improbable high-altitude adventures continue until they reach their natural conclusion and it is time to come down.

And so to the end. In the lower reaches of the Panjshir, where the river thunders through a great gorge, Carless spots the Edwardian explorer Wilfred Thesiger and his motley caravan. The last three pages of the book build up to a magnificent crescendo dominated by the mid-forty-something Old Etonian surrounded by wooden presses and tin trunks marked 'British Museum'. One moment he is pondering his men's chances of survival ('That cook's going to die,' said Thesiger; 'hasn't got a coat and look at his feet'), the next he's channelling his inner curmudgeon ('England's going to pot') and finally he's reliving his triumphs as a self-appointed doctor.

'Do you do it? Cutting off fingers?'

'Hundreds of them,' he said dreamily, for it was very late. 'Lord, yes. Why the other day I took out an eye. I enjoyed that.'

They turn in for the night and Newby delivers his final flourish.

The ground was like iron with sharp rocks sticking up out of it. We started to blow up our air-beds. 'God, you must be a couple of pansies,' said Thesiger.

Given the pitiless, hysterical lampooning of Carless, perhaps it is just as well that Newby dedicated the book to his friend with a generous acknowledgement of his starring role. 'This book is dedicated to Hugh Carless of Her Majesty's Foreign Service, without whose determination, it must be obvious to anyone who reads it, this journey could never have been made.'

Although *Love and War in the Apennines*, the story of his wartime experiences in the Italian mountains, is generally considered a finer book, by both Newby fans and Newby himself, *A Short Walk in the Hindu Kush* thrust him decisively into the first rank of travel writers. After that false start in fashion, it put the afterburners on his career as a writer. Whether it performed the diplomatic equivalent for Carless of the Foreign Office must surely be a moot point.

JUSTIN MAROZZI is planning to return to the Panjshir with a favourite travel companion, this time bearing in mind how Newby dealt with Carless. You can also hear him taking a literary journey through North Africa and the Middle East on our podcast, Episode 21, 'A Bookshelf in Tripoli'.

An Appetite for Looking

ALEXANDRA HARRIS

'Is Pevsner in the back?' A familiar question from the driver when setting off for almost any destination in England – familiar not from my childhood (I don't think there were Pevsners at home) but from years of adult friendship with people interested in buildings and places. Yes, here is *Leicestershire* in the footwell, and the seat pocket yields *Nottinghamshire*, which may mean that instead of driving straight past Hickling (say) we'll take time to look at the 'unusually rewarding number of engraved C18 and early C19 slate headstones in the churchyard'. If the church door is open we'll find art of every century inside, from the 'wild interlacing' of a carved Saxon coffin to the 'poor box, small, 1685, but still not at all classical'. We'll even notice the door hinges on the way out, enjoying the extravagance of the medieval ironwork. Pevsner calls them 'accomplished'.

Who was this man who had such a passion for detail that he paid attention to door hinges, yet who thought and worked on such a colossal scale that he wrote thirty-two volumes in *The Buildings of England* series single-handedly? I first read Susie Harries's mighty *Nikolaus Pevsner* when it came out in 2011 and remember the fascination of starting to understand Pevsner's early life in Germany, the influences on his approach to art, and the extraordinary motivation that kept him writing, lecturing, campaigning and sitting on myriad committees in the intervals between visiting buildings in whichever county he was currently researching. Sometimes an individual life

---

Susie Harries, *Nikolaus Pevsner: The Life* (2011), is out of print but we can obtain second-hand copies.

story seems to tell, with particular clarity, the refracted history of a century. To an extent I hadn't expected (having associated him mainly with rood screens and accomplished ironwork) Pevsner's life – as told by Harries – was one of those.

Harries's book won the Wolfson History Prize (sharing the honour with another exceptional work long in the making, *The Reformation of the Landscape* by Alexandra Walsham). Then, as always, new titles came to take its place on the front tables and off it went to await the specialists who would seek it out. But this biography took twenty years to complete and was made to last. Like Pevsner's own books it struck me as enormously informative, eccentric, practical and straight-talking all at once, concerned with the big questions lurking under the detail, and with equipping readers to make up their own minds. I might never read all 800 pages again but I knew I'd be back.

And here I am, prompted partly by the succession of revised *Buildings of England* volumes appearing with impressive regularity from Yale University Press. The project to update the whole series is now reaching its culmination, so that recent months have brought *Durham, Hampshire, Wiltshire* and others – each much enlarged from the first editions of Pevsner's time, shiny black spines binding together judicious summings-up of great cathedrals, Victorian suburbs, market squares. Each book is a vote of faith in Pevsner's legacy, re-equipping his work for the present. I scan the new entries, looking for what's changed, feeling the vitality of this national institution that gathers obscure and famed places into alphabetical order and puts knowledge of their buildings in our hands.

It's only vital, however, if it matters to the next generations too. Does it? Will it? Enquiries among students in their twenties yield blank faces: 'Pevsner' means neither a man nor a guidebook. As I start to explain, I worry that I'm describing a pleasantly irrelevant line in pew-related pedantry, the sort of thing loved by people of a certain milieu in the 1970s. I go home, read Susie Harries and start the conversation again with conviction.

Nikolaus Pevsner reveals, I think, an extraordinarily strenuous and open-minded thinker. He was an internationalist who cared about national cultures, an antiquarian who was also an acute and committed advocate of contemporary design. Never entirely at home in England, he wrote without any hint of complacency or shared assumptions; he was concentrating and on his mettle. Old and new, rural and urban, domestic and commercial: all these drew his serious consideration. A shopfront in Coventry could interest him as much as a carved font in a Cornish hamlet: either might provoke excitement or dismay. Nor did he skimp on attention to the kinds of town so often overlooked by those preferring the countryside or the city – places that are now being encouraged towards regeneration through the 'Towns Fund' (though there's little agreement about what kind of regenerated future they should aim for). For these reasons, all of which are to do with breadth of vision converging with respect for the small-scale, local and immediate, Pevsner's voice may prove both bracing and heartening as we try to invent our post-pandemic environment. Or we might simply be glad of a Pevsner volume in the footwell or holdall as we head off on staycations.

We're lucky to have these books, which exist only because the Nazis' rise to power in 1933 brought disaster for a young art historian lecturing at the University of Göttingen. Nikolaus Pevsner had grown up in Leipzig, in a cultured and comfortably well-off Russian-Jewish family, though he was rarely comfortable as a child himself, pouring his agonized self-scrutiny into diaries and plays. He found direction and hope when he started to learn about the history of art, and to discover modern architecture with its space and rationality – so different from the highly furnished and emotionally fraught family apartment. All his life he would be a man of intense emotions and rationalism, constantly managing these aspects of himself and putting them to use.

He was getting a foothold as a scholar and working all hours to support his wife Lola and three children when the implications of

Nazism became clear to him. He had been slow to see it coming, and some of the tutors he continued to admire were Nazi sympathizers. He has been much criticized as a result, and Harries tackles the situation head-on. 'What exactly did Pevsner's political views amount to in the 1930s?', she asks, and then gives a nuanced reading of the evidence. There was no nuance at all in Nazi Germany's treatment of Pevsner. As an ethnic Jew (he had long since converted to Protestantism, though he never practised a faith of any sort) he was banned from lecturing, and then ejected from the university altogether. His dreams of following in the great German historical tradition fell apart. He loved his country and its art, and he had no choice but to leave. He went first to Italy, hoping to find a job there. If he had, we might now possess *The Buildings of Umbria* rather than *Lincolnshire*. Instead it was in England that narrow opportunities opened. Only after two years of graft was he settled enough for Lola and the children to come, very reluctantly, and join him.

Pevsner's descendants gave Harries access to all his personal papers. One trunk was labelled in Pevsner's hand: 'Mr Thief. This is not locked. It contains nothing of value.' To his biographer, of course, its contents were of inestimable worth. Even so, Harries knows that a great deal is missing. He threw away forty years' worth of his enormous private diary (or *hefchten*), the volumes covering the whole of his marriage. Whatever intimacies and discords were written there, he had the discretion to put them beyond reach.

It's not only in the astonishing reams of candid personal writing that Harries is able to trace Pevsner's responses to the tribulations of his own life and of European history. A subtle portrait of him emerges from her readings of his published work on art and architecture. In *Pioneers of Modern Design* (1936), the book that made his name, he claimed William Morris as the great originator of the modern movement, whose emphasis on form, craft and function laid the groundwork for the radically new architecture of Walter Gropius, one of Pevsner's German heroes. Without being remotely autobiographical, this is a book full of personal significance. Pevsner was making sense of his new life in England, establishing the interrelatedness of European cultures, championing modern ideas that the English often regarded as alien. 'The modern movement was somewhere he felt at home,' writes Harries. That simple insight has been on my mind for a decade. Architecture that might feel to others unhomely spoke to Pevsner of his past and of belonging.

In 1946, Pevsner told Allen Lane, founder of Penguin, about Georg Dehio's catalogue of historic German buildings, published in five volumes between 1905 and 1912. Shouldn't there be an equivalent in England? he wondered aloud. With Lane's consent the giant scheme was begun. I'm glad to understand the German roots of the project, and its ambition to make clear both the uniqueness of English buildings and their place in the broad currents of European art.

Harries's descriptions of Pevsner's county tours are a joy, though it might not have been such a pleasure to be on the road with him. He set a relentless pace – no long pub lunches or diversions to the seaside. His lists of items to pack are superbly evocative of the mobile office ('paper clips (large); pins; foolscap . . . second fountain pen'), the hours spent inspecting dark churches ('torch; 100-watt bulb; aspirin') and the hurried stopovers ('drip-dry shirts . . . tin opener'). Some counties he visited alone, doing all the driving (which he hated), organizing historical notes for each building, making arrangements with hundreds of house-owners and key-holders, and writing up his text each evening. The process worked much better when Lola was at the wheel and could make arrangements for the following day while Pevsner was writing. Starting in Cornwall in 1948, with Lola driving an Austin Ten on loan from Penguin, and continuing until her sudden death in 1963, they worked on the recording of England. Their last county together was *Yorkshire*. Pevsner referred to his later work as 'after my time', as if, without her, he was posthumous.

Through the post-war decades he held multiple university posts, lectured to packed halls and acquired legendary status as a teacher.

He was loved and revered by students at Birkbeck, Cambridge and the Courtauld Institute, many of whom felt decisively shaped by his influence. He didn't need to keep on teaching; it might have been shed to make more time for the books and influential committee work. But he believed in the power of lectures to open up new ideas for students, and in the accruing, argumentative work of a class talking together. Harries quotes some of his Courtauld exam questions: 'Analyse the spread of "Caravaggism" outside Italy.' 'Which do you consider to have been the more influential artist, Manet or William Morris?' Doubtless I'd flunk this test, but the provocative turns of phrase, the specific yet openly exploratory tasks, make me want to set a timer and begin. Think of the giant considerations lying latent in those questions: what *is* influence and how does it relate to value? How do ideas travel? Really, how does culture *work*?

The Buildings of England volumes were another kind of teaching. They were always intended for the general public, and when he really wanted to do things well Pevsner preferred to think of the child who might read him rather than the professor. His aspiration was for 'every schoolboy to have his own volume of his own county in his pocket', so that he might start to place himself in England and in Europe, and to develop what Harries calls simply and rightly 'an appetite for looking'. Not many of today's schoolchildren have their own county volume, but some would derive a great deal from it if they did.

One last thought lingers after rereading Harries's portrait of this prodigiously productive man with his coherent individual vision. She shows how consistently Pevsner thought beyond individuals to wider movements, or to 'the spirit of an age'. He thought beyond himself as well. He wanted *The Buildings of England* series to exist but it did not belong to him. He meant it when he spoke of the *Kent* volume, which he had delegated to John Newman, as the best in the series. When he advertised for additions and corrections, he welcomed them. He was a truly collaborative thinker. The expanded and rewritten volumes now appearing are still 'Pevsners' in the sense that this is just what he had hoped for. So in 2022 Pevsner is still 'in the back' and also out in front, drawing our attention to what surrounds us, sharpening our appetite for looking. I'm putting Harries's superb biography where I can easily find it again. It shows, in abundance, why he matters.

ALEXANDRA HARRIS lives in Oxford and is writing about West Sussex, a county that Pevsner delegated to Ian Nairn. She runs the 'Arts of Place' network at the University of Birmingham. You can also hear her talking about winter in literature on our podcast, Episode 26, 'A Winter's Tale'.

Academic Affairs

RACHEL COOKE

People tend to overstate the case when it comes to fiction and empathy: just as there are lots of nasty writers, there are also plenty of insensitive, clod-hopping readers. But still, novels can be pretty useful for teenagers trying to understand the behaviour of certain adults.

In my case, the adults in question were my parents. To be more specific, one of my parents: my father, a man I loved half to death, but whose behaviour was – how to put this? – on the errant side. I was always trying to work him out, but the problem was that I knew no one else quite like him. My friends' fathers liked washing their cars and mowing their lawns, and never did anything remotely out of the ordinary. My father, however, might have been beamed down from another planet. I would look at him – at this point, you need to picture a small, bearded man in Dr Scholl sandals worn with (horrors) socks, a look which a lot of women seemed to find unaccountably sexy – and wonder at the state of the heart that seemed to be beating so very rapidly beneath his corduroy jacket.

It was this conundrum that led the young me to campus novels for, yes, my father was an academic. The first such novel that I read – devoured would be a better word – was David Lodge's *Changing Places*, borrowed from the sixth-form library, where contraband books with 'adult' themes were to be found if you looked hard enough. In an instant I recognized its hero, frisky Professor Zapp, as having been cut from the same cloth as my dad.

Alison Lurie, *The War Between the Tates* (1974)
Vintage · Pb · 368pp · £9.99 · ISBN 9781784876265

Naturally, this soon led me to Malcolm Bradbury's *The History Man*, in which a sociology lecturer called Howard Kirk is told that his promiscuity may lead to his being sacked for 'gross moral turpitude'. Kirk, pompous and somewhat foolish, was very different from my father, who was funny and smart. But his *appetites* were all too familiar, and after this, there was no stopping me. I had found a rich literary seam, and I was determined to mine it, usually while sitting in an oak tree on my father's allotment. As he considered his beloved kale (long before kale was fashionable) I would sit on my branch, utterly absorbed by bed-hopping eggheads and their fictional universities. These novels were for me the literary equivalent of *I-Spy* books. In their pages, you could find every species of clever, over-sexed bloke. *Yep, seen that one,* I'd think, picturing some wiry-haired colleague of my dad's. Slowly, the adult world was beginning to make more sense.

It was a little while after this that I discovered Alison Lurie. At university I met J, still my closest female friend. Having bonded over our bolter, brain-box fathers – my dad was by now married to his fourth wife – she recommended *Foreign Affairs*, Lurie's 1984 Pulitzer Prize winner. Of course I adored it. Its message, which has to do with the way in which being loved alters a person, moved me then, as it moves me now.

But this piece is not about *Foreign Affairs*, a book that is easy to love. It is about the novel of Lurie's that I read next, *The War Between the Tates*, a rather spikier proposition. As it happens, *The War Between the Tates* was published in 1974, the very same year that my father departed the family home for a love nest – translation: a small, terraced house – with one of his former students. This, obviously, is one reason why I cherished it.

At its heart is a similar affair. But when I read it again recently, I found it powerful and striking in other ways too. It is a brilliant book, not only about university life, rarefied and febrile, but also about such things as middle age, motherhood and feminism. Above all, it captures something of what it is like to live in the midst of a culture war, when no one wants to be on the 'wrong' side and when even the smallest utterance may be misconstrued. This seems to me to give it a weird new life at this point in the twenty-first century – for all that so many hippies with dirty feet appear among its pages.

Like *Foreign Affairs* its setting is Corinth University, a thinly disguised version of Cornell. When it begins, it is 8.15 in the morning in a lovely old house not far from the university, and Erica Tate, a sometime illustrator, is sitting with her head on the kitchen table, weeping. Why are her teenage children, she wonders, so horrible? It is, she thinks, as if she is 'keeping a boarding house in a bad dream'. Meanwhile, in his office on campus, her political scientist husband, Brian Tate, nervously awaits the arrival of a graduate student called Wendy Gahaghan. For the third time, he is about to try and break up with this poor girl. This won't be easy. Wendy, who favours suede mini-dresses and an excess of beads, and who believes in such notions as astral projection, is, just like the rest of her (to Brian, slightly terrifying) generation, seemingly hell-bent on sexual freedom. The words 'my wife has found out' have no meaning for Wendy.

What follows – all of it expertly controlled by Lurie – has elements of farce. Events will conspire to ensure that Brian, no matter how weaselly, cannot, after all, wriggle out of his (non) commitment to Wendy. Worse, his own wife will play a part in his fate; feminism, of which he has lately heard so much, now bites him on the bum, moving from mere theory into practical application.

Newly liberated, albeit against her will, Erica will now also take a lover: Zed, the drippy proprietor of the Krishna Bookshop that is the bane of Brian's life (Wendy, you see, regards Zed as her guru). As in any war, many deals must be broken, and many alliances made. On Erica's side is pugnacious Danielle, another academic who has recently separated from her husband, the waspish literary critic Leonard Zimmern. But the battle between the Tates is, the reader comes to realize, just one skirmish in a wider war. Corinth University, like the rest of America in the era of Vietnam, is in turmoil. Students are protesting against, among other things, Brian's reactionary colleague Professor Dibble, a character who may or may not have been based on the noted young philosopher and classicist Allen Bloom – and when Brian gets mixed up in their demonstration, he makes an utter berk of himself.

At her best, Lurie is properly funny. No one in her world is safe from a skewering; having slowly marinated her characters, she then barbecues them for our delectation. But she is all wisdom and tenderness too. 'You have already made your choices, taken the significant moral actions of your life long ago when you were inexperienced,' she writes of middle-aged women like Erica in *The War Between the Tates*. 'Now you have more knowledge of yourself and the world; you are equipped to make choices, but there are none left to make.' She is particularly good on the sex lives of the long-married and the newly separated; her careful, gentle paragraphs capture emotions (and embarrassments) that, though often felt, are still rarely expressed.

If *The War Between the Tates* is a book about a divorce, and all the terrible rancour that comes with such a rupture, it's also about renewal, a process that must involve, somewhere along the way, forgiveness – something that applies, in the book, to the shifting sands of politics as much as it does to relationships.

Which brings me back to my father, with whom I was often furious as a girl, but of whom I now think – he died in 2004 – only with deep gratitude and an indulgent amusement that is the best kind of love. Getting to this state took, I'll admit, quite a long time; I had to sleepwalk into my own emotional muddles before I was able to stop playing the puritan. But Lurie, I think, also played her part. Her universe was, and is, deeply meaningful to me: ever sprightly and jumbled, but brimful, too, of understanding and abiding good sense.

RACHEL COOKE is a writer and columnist at the *Observer*, and the television critic of the *New Statesman*. She is currently working on a new book, *The Reckoning*, which explores ideas around bad behaviour and good art.

Unsuspected Depths

GRANT MCINTYRE

My sister gave me *Copsford* (1948). It was clearly a book she loved, and its author – Walter Murray – was someone we'd once known. So it seemed odd I'd never heard of it. It's a strange, exhilarating book about a solitary year spent wholly absorbed in the natural world – a book in the tradition that runs from Richard Jefferies to Robert Macfarlane and perhaps has roots in Wordsworth too, and John Clare in saner moments. But though it has devotees and is reissued now and then, it has never been widely read. In fact most people, like me, have never heard of it.

Walter Murray was born in 1900. He was bright and maybe optimistic too, war having ended, and in 1919 he moved to London to become a journalist. Newspapers however proved the wrong world for him, and London seemed a kind of death. He couldn't bear its grey streets, crowds and haste. Indoor work meant clouds and sunlight passed unseen, and the four seasons merged into one. His work depressed him and so did his room, a third-floor back 'with its tiny gas fire, its naked electric light and its distressing view'. One winter evening by the Thames he watched the smoke 'roll sombrely away from the four black satanic chimneys of the power station [with] the dull fire of sunset trapped among them'. He called it the dramatic setting of enslaved humanity and quit.

It must have been hard to go home worsted by his first job. But he did – to Horam in Sussex, to start afresh. Horam was an unprepos-

Walter J. C. Murray, *Copsford* (1948)
Little Toller · Pb · 168pp · £14 · ISBN 9781908213709

sessing village by a railway station, though surrounded by glorious fields and woods. It was also where his 'music mistress' lived, a young pianist who was his girlfriend in the tentative way of those times. He didn't exactly start again, but the following year did transform his life. It began quixotically but became something more profound.

*

I want to fast-forward briefly to the Walter Murray who was part of my sister's life and my own. In his mid-twenties he and his music mistress, by then his wife, started a village school and that's where, years later, we began our education. Murray's was the only school our parents would contemplate for us. It was private but inexpensive and I'm not sure they'd noticed how unconventional it was. I started early, aged 3, because my sister aged 5 refused to go without me. She was my keeper and, remarkably for a girl of 5, had already taught me to read and told me solemnly all about sex.

From this distance it feels as if school life was mostly Sports Days, with the whole village involved. I seem to remember bands of pupils in white tunics marching from the corners of the playing field, shouting slogans and waving banners and – as I thought at the time – pretending to be ancient Greeks. A whole circus of sports was compèred by Mr Murray with his loudhailer. At the end there would be a tremendous climactic tea in the hall.

The school did pantomimes too, and plays, most written by Mr Murray himself. Also concerts; Mrs Murray would play the piano, he the violin, and capable pupils would play or sing. There was plenty of nature study as well, walks and fact-finding both near and far. And there was also a strong academic tradition, sometimes eccentric. I remember being taught simple French, pronouncing the words as if they were English so as not to be confused by too much Frenchness – a novel system which might have worked, except that the teacher fell over a log in the field and wasn't seen again.

Away from the commotion of school there was a nature sanctuary in the grounds; it was completely hushed except for the birds. Trusty pupils were allowed in, but silence was too difficult for me. The Murrays had a son who died at 15 of meningitis. No one spoke of this grief, but the sanctuary was his memorial.

I have lively images of both: he vigorous but gentle and a bit reserved; she thoughtful, getting a little stout, chignon always about to come down; and in early days happy to tie my shoes up for me. The school took pupils to 18; it was a completely engaging experience. But after a few years we were sent to stuffier, more humdrum schools – perhaps for the best. I think my sister has missed it ever since.

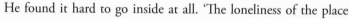

The new start in Horam that Murray devised in 1919 was not a school but something much less social. He planned to find wild herbs and sell them to specialist firms for use in medicines. These were (to me at least) strange herbs: clivers, centaury, agrimony, traveller's joy, eyebright, yarrow and so on. His first need was to find somewhere isolated and above all cheap, where he could live alone, repair his psyche and seek out the plants that would pay for his keep. Amazingly, the music mistress had heard there was indeed an empty cottage not far off, Copsford. But it was a shock when he saw it. It was no bucolic welcome; in fact it was twenty years derelict, bare and grim like a rock in a sea of rough grass, its grey chimney stark against the skyline.

He found it hard to go inside at all. 'The loneliness of the place  repelled me, repelled me forcibly, and I would gladly have left it in peace and forever had I not needed just such a place.' The first moments beyond the door were 'graven so deep in my memory that I think nothing can ever efface them. It was as though the place resented intrusion, as though human life had no further right there.' Next there was 'a scampering, which grew louder, a violent crescendo of hurrying multitudes, a crash . . . and then stillness.

A stillness more terrifying than any movement . . . It required a great effort even to breathe and a concentration of will-power to relax muscles which held me as rigid as a dead stick.'

In his biography, *The Green Man of Horam*, Tom Wareham wonders whether the sense of hostility and the swarms of rats weren't to some extent symptoms of Murray's state of mind. The rats at their most melodramatic were always somehow in the walls. And his dog Floss, bought from the postman, seemed to banish them altogether just by keeping him company. Patrick Leigh Fermor wrote of similar feelings on going into a monastery as a guest, to write a book: 'the place assumed the character of an enormous tomb', he said, and 'a mood of depression and of unspeakable loneliness felled me like a hammer-stroke'. But it didn't do so for long, and so it was for Murray too. He would somehow force himself to tame the place and clean it up. There might be no proper door, no unbroken window or watertight roof, but there was a well, and also a pond in which he could wash. It would never be fit for habitation, but he would inhabit it anyway.

It helped that the countryside around was an enchanted place. Alien as it was, the cottage stood on what was almost an island between the little River Darn and one of its tributaries, reached by a barred footbridge as if it were a tiny independent state. And what was extremely rare about it was that there was no longer any track or path that led there.

The farmer who owned it was suspicious but agreed: 3 shillings a week, with milk and eggs, plus the right to wander anywhere on his land. So Murray set to work. 'There is a fascination about herb-gathering,' he wrote, 'which I felt from the very first day. It is not merely the satisfaction of having gathered something good and useful . . . not merely the atavistic urge to harvest, not only the close contact with Nature, but something of all three, mingled with the delights of liberty.' He learned to read plantscapes and soon could find his herbs however well concealed. He could duck behind the tapestries hanging from fallen boughs, and negotiate impenetrable jungles of brambles, nettles and thistles.

I travelled by spinney and copse, through shaw and forgotten corduroy, at first because there I expected to find my herbs, but later because I became secretive and shy. Living so close to the wild, almost instinctively I copied creatures from the wild. I travelled swiftly, silently and unseen. I learned woodland behaviour, I heard woodland sounds.

He became rather mystical:

The freedom that I won by living in that lonely cottage brought me into touch with real Nature in a way that I had never understood to be possible . . . It was closer contact than touch, it was almost union . . . The birds, animals, trees, plants, insects, all meant or brought something to my life. I felt their presence . . . I became more sensitive to light, my sense of smell brought me new contact, movement was language.

Then more mystical still:

At rare moments in our lives, we are suddenly aware of an altogether new world, different completely from that in which we normally live . . . For brief moments we perceive meaning instead of things. In those golden minutes I understood every word on a single page of the magic book of Life inscribed in a language neither written nor spoken.

Inevitably the harvesting year ended and with it the hunting and euphoria. He bagged up the dried herbs and put them on the train to his dealers in London – bribing the guard to care for them like children. After some time a cheque arrived, for £34 4s 2d. It was modest but would do to live on. What would not do, he realized, was the fact that it was money. The things he'd suffered, learned and done were part of him; the herbs had grown in their idiosyncratic ways; he had picked them with restraint, skilfully dried them in the now aromatic rooms of the cottage, and shipped them with love. And all this had turned into a little slip of coloured paper. He realized there was no bridge between the idyll and a lived life. He'd needed his solitary existence, but it had to end.

Arrival at Copsford had been hard, and now departure was too. Rain came down suddenly, with maximum force and all day long. The little rivers became two vast sheets of swirling water, fizzing from the force of the downpour. Dependable way-markers vanished beneath the surface.

> I stared at this bewildering sight, thinking I must be crazy . . . It could not be.
>
> I stripped on the shores of the flood. Holding my clothes in a bundle before me, I waded out into the icy, racing waters. I found the barred bridge and somehow crossed it. The water was breast high on the other side and I had difficulty keeping my feet, but at last I was across. I wedged my clothes in a bush and returned for Floss. Somehow we crossed the frothing waters at the bridge and then Floss swam the rest.
>
> I stood, a naked man, in the midst of the floods; leaves, mud, froth, ice, swirled past me. I looked up the hill through the streaming rain and could just see the top of that grey chimney. Unmistakably, Copsford had returned to its former self. And back in civilization was the music mistress.

As I read it, *Copsford* seemed like some medieval allegory, written perhaps by the poet of *Sir Gawain*. Guided from afar by his damsel (who sometimes brought him cakes), a poor knight braved despair to reach a mystical land of enlightenment, then fought his way back to the human world, healed. Our Mr Murray of Murray's school was that healed man, though naturally at the time my sister and I had no idea.

*

Though he never achieved much fame as a writer, Murray did do so on the wireless. The three wise men of early nature broadcasting were Peter Scott, Maxwell Knight and Walter J. C. Murray. Scott was the son of the Antarctic hero and named after Peter Pan, the creation of his father's estranged but still close friend J. M. Barrie. He was a painter, an inventor, an Olympic medallist and the founder of Slimbridge. Maxwell Knight was the model for James Bond's M, though unlike M he thought animal study was the key to spy-craft. He had once been a bandleader, was fascinated by the occult and drawn to fascism. And Murray was a schoolmaster with strange unsuspected depths.

GRANT MCINTYRE was to some extent formed by the hero of this piece. Much later he became a publisher, and then a sculptor, and is now mostly an idler.

Of Captains and Khans

LESLEY DOWNER

Many years ago, when it was possible to do such things, I hitchhiked to India. I travelled through Iran and Afghanistan, saw the Great Buddhas at Bamiyan, and rode through the Khyber Pass on the roof of a brilliantly painted truck with my hair blowing in the wind. Later, as the world changed and carefree travel became more difficult, I came across Peter Hopkirk's *The Great Game* (1990) and was thrilled to read about the adventures of the first western travellers to those regions in the nineteenth century.

Of course, those travellers were more serious-minded than I was, and their travels were often a matter of life or death. The young men (they were invariably men) whose tales Hopkirk tells, mainly British and Russian, operated in Central Asia and up into the Pamirs as explorers, spies, mapmakers, soldiers, and often all four at once. Many wrote books which Hopkirk brilliantly synthesizes, describing their successes, scrapes and disasters, and he also dug deep into Foreign Office and other archives. It's gripping, page-turning stuff, as colourfully written as fiction, with a cliff-hanger at the end of each chapter. It's also a revelatory depiction of the behaviour of the colonizing powers in an era when they believed the world was theirs for the taking – and of some of the occasions on which they met with their comeuppance.

The story encompasses places that I was fortunate enough to visit some years after that first youthful trip, such as the marvellous cities

Peter Hopkirk, *The Great Game: On Secret Service in High Asia* (1990)
John Murray · Pb · 592pp · £12.99 · ISBN 9780719564475

of the Silk Road. It begins with Prince Alexander Bekovich, sent by Peter the Great in 1717 to propose an alliance with the Khan of the glorious, pink-walled city of Khiva. The Khan however had other ideas. Many years later my Khivan guide Ali gleefully showed me the place on the Great Gate where Bekovich's head had been hung.

The impassable deserts and mountain wastes of Central Asia separated two great empires – that of Russia to the north and, to the south, India, held by the British East India Company, a formidable force with its own army, until it was dissolved in 1858 and India became the jewel in the crown of the British Empire. For the British the great question was whether a Russian army might cross these harsh expanses and swoop down to take India. Both they and the Russians also wanted to find new markets for trade and to expand their territory and spheres of influence. This made it vital to map these vast regions and negotiate their way around the potentates who ruled them.

It was a daunting task, one which needed a specific sort of person to attempt it. You had to be young, fearless, hugely resourceful and so fluent in at least some of the languages of the region that even native speakers wouldn't realize that you were an intruder, while fully aware that if you were caught your government would disown you. You also had to be familiar with eastern protocol. Lashings of charm were a useful attribute. And sometimes, as in the case of Bekovich, you might have all these qualities and still they wouldn't save you.

The earliest British adventurers, Captain Charles Christie and Lieutenant Henry Pottinger, satisfied all these requirements. Setting out in 1810 to explore the unmapped deserts of Baluchistan, Christie disguised himself as a Tartar horse-dealer, this being a world where horses were all-important and horse-dealers, it seems, two a penny. It took all his resources to avoid exposure which, as Hopkirk reminds us, meant instant death. Eventually he reached the spectacular walled city of Herat, the first westerner ever to do so. He described the villages and gardens with admiration but, as a military man, he thought the city's multiple moats and massive walls 'very contemptible as a fortification'.

Meanwhile the 20-year-old Pottinger, disguised as a holy man, had set off on a 900-mile journey across Baluchistan and Persia, travelling through the gruelling deserts of Helmand and Kerman. He had a close shave when a boy in a remote village, who happened to have seen the only European ever to have passed that way before, commented that this supposed holy man looked just like him. Pottinger and Christie finally met up again in Persia, safe ground at that time.

In many cases intrepid young Russians were the first to reach these distant fabled lands. The first to visit Khiva after Bekovich's ill-fated venture was the 24-year-old Captain Nikolai Muraviev. He arrived in 1819, having joined a camel train disguised as a Turcoman to cross the Karakum desert. He described the prosperous villages surrounding the palaces and well-tended gardens of the rich in Khiva and 'the great mosque rising above the city's forty-foot-high walls, its blue-tiled dome, surmounted by a massive golden ball, shimmering in the sunlight'. The Khan, he wrote, was six foot tall with a short red beard and spoke 'distinctly, fluently and with dignity'.

In describing these adventures Hopkirk conjures up caravans of thousands of camels and hundreds of men, crossing and recrossing the desert sands in a stream of traffic so dense that travellers like Muraviev had to wait for the whole train to pass before moving on. The deserts themselves formed a natural barrier – terrible heat in summer, brutal cold in winter, which in 1840 forced a Russian army advancing on Khiva to turn back after losing nearly all its men and camels in one of the worst winters ever experienced.

Besides the men on the ground and the Emirs and Khans with whom they crossed paths, the Great Game players included generals and officers, both British and Russian, and the powerbrokers back home who made the decisions. A change of government or of alliances could render a man's work meaningless overnight, while instructions from government might wreck the delicate network of relationships that the spies had painstakingly built up on the ground.

A poignant case is that of the mysterious Captain Yan Vitkevich, whom Henry Rawlinson, a young British subaltern, met in 1837 while travelling through the remote borderlands of eastern Persia. Vitkevich's mission was to woo Dost Mohammed, the formidable Emir of Kabul who wielded power over Afghanistan, the chief bulwark between Russia and British India. The British officer Alexander Burnes beat him to it and became great friends with the potentate. But as a result of policy decisions back home, Vitkevich found his star rising while that of Burnes fell.

Then, virtually overnight, the relationship between Britain and Russia changed again. Unsuspecting, Vitkevich returned to St Petersburg having achieved everything he'd been charged with, including a treaty with Dost Mohammed. But far from being rewarded, he was cold-shouldered. The Foreign Minister Nesselrode declared that he knew of no such Captain Vitkevich – 'except for an adventurer of that name, who had lately been engaged in some unauthorized intrigues in Kabul and Kandahar'. Vitkevich returned to his hotel room, burned his papers and shot himself.

Burnes was another casualty of the swings and roundabouts of government policy. To him Kabul was a paradise, with gardens full of fruit trees and songbirds. In 1836 he established a permanent mission there. But then things started to go wrong. He was forced to relay increasingly hostile and insulting messages from the British government, which finally decided to send in troops to replace Dost Mohammed with his more malleable – and useless – half-brother. In the uprising that followed, Burnes was torn apart by a furious mob and the British garrison, attempting to flee to the safety of Jalalabad, was massacred on the road.

Another salutary tale is that of Colonel Charles Stoddart, who failed to observe eastern protocol. When he arrived in Bokhara he happened to cross paths with the Emir, Nasrullah. Instead of dismounting he saluted the Emir from his horse, an unforgivable breach of etiquette. Shortly afterwards he was thrown into a vermin-filled pit where he stayed until his colleague, Captain Arthur Conolly, arrived to attempt to rescue him. Both men ended up being executed in the public square under the ramparts of Bokhara's great Ark citadel, where today you can still see their cells.

This Great Game, as it was known (it was Conolly who first coined the phrase), was one of incredibly high stakes, as British and Russian, Westerner and Asian pitted their wits against each other. It was marked by many moments of high drama but also by moments of comedy, as when Burnes met the Grand Vizier of Bokhara, 'a wizened old man with small crafty eyes and a long grey beard'. Feigning innocence, the vizier asked him if Christians ate pork. Burnes was ready. 'Only the poor,' he replied. Next the crafty vizier asked what it tasted like. Replied Burnes, 'I have *heard* that it is like beef.' As Burnes was leaving, the vizier had one last request: to bring him 'a good pair of English spectacles' if he ever returned.

Little by little the deserts of Central Asia were mapped and the Russians took over the great city states of the region – Khokand, Bokhara, Khiva and finally the fabled city of Merv. The field of play then expanded. The British now worried that the Russians might invade India through the supposedly impassable mountains of the Pamirs and sent men out to survey them surreptitiously.

Adventurers like Lieutenant Francis Younghusband headed for once legendary places like Hunza where, high up in the mountains, he met the Russian agent Captain Gromchevsky who entertained him with a fine dinner and plenty of vodka – one of several occasions when Briton and Russian dined together, knowing that the following day they would be adversaries again.

Younghusband's mission was to form an alliance with the ruler, Safdar Ali. The problem was that Ali assumed 'that the Empress of India [Queen Victoria], the Czar of Russia and the Emperor of China were chiefs of neighbouring tribes'. Most of these khans and emirs had little idea of the strength of the great armies who were encroaching on their territory.

The Great Game is the story of how much of Asia as we know it today was made, often as a result of misunderstandings, as the British tried to thwart what they suspected was a Russian advance and the Russians reacted to the moves they saw the British making, each trying to outfox the other. Far from seeing the great cities and states of Central Asia and the Pamirs as ancient kingdoms with fascinating cultures, the British and Russians viewed them solely in terms of their strategic value and regarded their monarchs as either troublesome or compliant. If troublesome they had no compunction in replacing them irrespective of the wishes of the people or the ability of the ruler, as in the case of Dost Mohammed.

The Great Game is of its time. Unlike modern scholars, Hopkirk used only English sources or sources translated from the Russian. No Russian primary sources are cited, nor are any from Afghanistan or the various Central Asian states, which also of course had their own cultures and histories. Nonetheless it's an incredibly gripping, brilliantly written, unputdownable read.

As to what would come to pass in this region – that was beyond any of these stalwart adventurers' wildest dreams.

LESLEY DOWNER is a writer, novelist, historian and inveterate traveller. She is half Chinese and has spent chunks of her life in India, Japan, China and points east.

Boxing Days

ANDREW RYAN

It is a great thrill to feel that all that separates you from the early
Victorians is a series of punches on the nose.

The jab that crunched into my nose before I had my guard up was a
fine lesson in the importance of being prepared, but it is not a fond
memory. Getting punched rarely is. A. J. Liebling, however, treasured
the blow he received from 'Philadelphia' Jack O'Brien, an American
pugilist already in his prime when Liebling was born in 1904. Liebling
saw the punch as a precious relic, linking him to O'Brien's era and the
eras before that. Just think of the greats who had punched O'Brien, the
greats who had punched them and so on back in time. Liebling was
proud to be part of such a passage of punches.

Abbot Joseph Liebling, who hated Abbot and went by the name
of Joe, owed his affluent childhood of governesses and European
travel to fur. His Austrian furrier father had turned the nothing he'd
arrived with in New York in the 1880s into a fortune. Liebling was,
according to one school, a 'pudgy, precocious and intellectual' boy.
His career began at the *Evening Bulletin* in Providence, Rhode Island,
but was interrupted in the summer of 1926 by a year of study at the
Sorbonne, a gift from his father. This deepened Liebling's Franco-
philia, if not his knowledge of his chosen subject, medieval literature.

In 1935, at the age of 31, having drifted through several newspapers, he joined the *New Yorker* as a staff writer and never left. He

A. J. Liebling, *The Sweet Science: Boxing and Boxiana – A Ring Side View* (1956)
Penguin · Pb · 256pp · £9.99 · ISBN 9780241343203

enjoyed his near three decades there, writing about politics, the press, sport, gastronomy, con men and plenty more. A tribute recalled that 'he could be heard humming and snorting with laughter as he pulled the sheets from his typewriter and read them over'. He earned the *Légion d'honneur* for his war reporting, landing under fire on Omaha Beach on D-Day. He was also the most committed of gourmands. But much as I delight in reading about a Liebling lunch of a dozen oysters, a beef-marrow-coated steak and two portions of cassoulet, I really turn to Liebling for his book on boxing, perhaps the greatest on pugilism ever written.

I am a civil servant who moonlights as a boxing writer, hopping from Whitehall meetings to York Hall beatings. When I first read Liebling, I was reporting on fights and feeling as if I was repeating old tales. The names and details might change but my characters and stories somehow stayed the same. *The Sweet Science* (1956), a collection of Liebling's essays on boxing written between 1951 and 1955, taught me to look beyond the main event. From a Chicago stadium to a 'monster' Dublin bus garage, Liebling follows the exploits of all-time greats, stolid journeymen and desperate no-hopers with enthusiasm and wit. Each essay is built around a single contest, but he uses that contest to report and reflect on a much wider world. Liebling's United States was, as it remains today, the centre of the boxing world and American fighters ruled the sport. At the start of the 1950s, fewer than one in ten American households had a television; by the decade's end, it was almost nine in ten. The boxing ring was a perfect fit for the small screen, and so a spectacle that had been for a few now became entertainment for millions.

Liebling would not be surprised that one of my more rewarding interviews was with a fledgling fighter perched on a giant plant pot in Spitalfields Market, for he had taught me that an honest admission is more likely to be found away from the formality of the press conference. The best line Liebling ever got from a boxer was overheard in a Syracuse bar in 1955. Billy Graham was a veteran, with over a hundred bouts behind him. After a narrow defeat, he called his mother. 'For such an old, ring-wise fellow,' Liebling reports, 'he sounded strangely like a small boy minimizing a bad school report . . . After listening to her for a bit, Graham said, "Oh sure. They're all satisfied. They all said I made a good try, but I guess it wasn't good enough."' He never fought again.

For the most part, however, Liebling wasn't interested in what boxers had to say. He knew well what I've learned painfully through hours of dull transcription: most boxers are skilled at delivering punches, but not at discussing the action. Instead, he sought out the company of the behind-the-scenes operators and gave their words more space than those of the stars. A manager steals the glory, an imposter in the first person as he claims his fighter's exploits as his own – 'Next time I'll knock him out quicker' – until of course his fighter loses. A matchmaker tells of how a heavyweight getting his first pay cheque is 'like a tiger tasting blood'. Long hours are spent at The Neutral Corner, the chosen New York bar for those operators and for retired boxers 'who favour a place where somebody is likely to recognize them'.

You always find yourself in bars with Liebling because he wrote about his whole night out. Strolling up to Madison Square Garden, he marvels at the 'men in shimmering gabardines and felt hats the colour of freshly unwrapped chewing gum, the women in spring suits and fur pieces'. He realizes that if he had watched the fight on TV he would have missed 'the prettiest lot of women I had seen in a long time'. As I hunt for a beer between bouts at Greenwich's O2 arena, I feel Liebling wouldn't think much of that slick but soulless venue. I know, however, that he'd have smiled at the shiny suits, sharp skirts and staggering stilettos on show. Some of us reporters are scruffier than our predecessors, but among the fans the dress code lives on.

Liebling was happier among the crowd than with the press. I lack his confidence to debate with fellow spectators who he felt were being loudly wrong. I do, however, share his faith in eavesdropping, knowing that the exclamations of excited punters can deliver colour that hardened hacks can't match. Joe Louis was the most famous boxer in the world and an American icon, but by 1951 he was well past his best and fighting on only for the money. Liebling watches him get knocked out by the soon-to-be great Rocky Marciano and hears a woman sobbing. Her puzzled boyfriend tells her that 'Rocky didn't do anything wrong.' The woman fires back: 'You're so cold. I hate you, too.' There's humour in their row: her seriousness, his confusion. But it also shows that however much we tell ourselves sport doesn't matter, it hurts to see our heroes fall, and in boxing they fall hard.

As a man who wrote about so much else Liebling never had to worry about being defined as 'just a sportswriter'. But he had no doubts about the sport's worth as a subject. He also knew that a sportswriter could and should do more than just record events, for boxing squeezes all of life into its rules and the ring, so a boxing writer is unlimited in his choice of subject. In describing a fighter's development as 'the growth of an artist', he isn't just claiming that boxers can be artists but also that sportswriters can write on art. That is a dizzying and thrilling claim for those of us who sometimes worry that we're only writing about two men in bright shorts.

Yet for all that Liebling wrote about scenes and ideas beyond the ring, a boxing writer must be judged on his performance between the ropes. Liebling himself earned his expertise through years of studious spectating and his images are evocative, wondrously improbable and very funny. Two battling boxers grunt with pleasure 'like hippopotamuses in a beer vat'. A featherweight is built 'like a bundle of loosely joined fishing poles, but they are apparently pickled bamboo'. A heavyweight sits down in his corner at the end of a difficult round 'as heavily as suet pudding upon the unaccustomed gastric system'.

Often, however, boxing isn't funny. For glory, money and the roar of the crowd, boxers risk their health and sometimes their lives. I know the sport's greatness, but I have moments when I wonder whether it ought to exist. I would have liked to ask Liebling how a man who so loved boxers could be seemingly untroubled by the moral compromise at boxing's core. He jokily dismissed the dangers to the brain on the evidence of that 'not particularly evasive boxer' Ernest Hemingway winning the Nobel Prize. Describing a badly injured boxer looking 'as though he had run into a nest of wild bees or fallen victim to instantaneous mumps' may be funny, but it's also cruel. If he had a moment's uncertainty, it never comes out on the page. Perhaps the sport was too deep in his blood for that.

Sitting in New York's 167th Street cafeteria in 1955, drinking tea and eating 'a smoked salmon sandwich on a soft onion roll', Liebling weighs up the fighters of the past against those of the present. He declares with pleasure that the 'world isn't going backward if you can just stay young enough to remember what it was really like when you were really young'. It would be far easier to join the grumpy legions, shaking their heads while speaking with misty eyes of a mythical golden age. But Liebling stays young and sees with the same fresh eye and sense of wonder that he had when he first fell for the sport. 'What would *Moby Dick* be if Ahab had succeeded? Just another fish story. The thing that is eternally diverting [about boxing] is the struggle of man against history – or what Albert Camus, who used to be an amateur middleweight, has called *The Myth of Sisyphus*.'

Liebling died eight years later, in 1963. He was only 59. The gourmand life had given him joy but also ill health. I wish he'd had one more decade and been able to see Muhammad Ali in his prime.

ANDREW RYAN is always in search of a ringside seat.

Fifty Years On

MICHAEL BARBER

If, as I did, you came of age in the Sixties, then one rite of passage you may have undergone was reading John Fowles's bestselling *Bildungsroman, The Magus* (1965), which provided, it was said, an experience 'beyond the literary' – in my case, a vicarious ego trip. How flattering to have so much time and energy expended in order to make you a better person! Even the indignant narrator, Nicholas Urfe, who compares what he's been through to 'exposure in the village stocks', can scarce forbear to cheer: 'that all this could be mounted just for me'.

But that was in another country. Returning to a book you've not opened for fifty-odd years is potentially as hazardous as meeting a long-lost lover. Furthermore, in his introduction to the revised edition (1977) – I had long since lost its predecessor – Fowles describes it as 'a novel of adolescence by a retarded adolescent'. Hardly a ringing endorsement. So why bother opening it again?

Partly because I had an argument with someone about the ending, and it didn't seem right to settle this by simply turning to the last few pages. But what clinched it was learning that Sam Mendes was proposing to adapt the book for television, a project that would certainly have delighted Fowles, who shared everyone's dismay at the

John Fowles, *The Magus* (1965: revised edition 1977)
Vintage · Pb · 672pp · £10.99 · ISBN 9780099478355
The original 1965 edition of *The Magus* is out of print as is Eileen Warburton's biography, *John Fowles: A Life in Two Worlds* (2004), but we can obtain second-hand copies of each.

disastrous film starring Michael Caine, whom he liked personally but thought 'totally incredible as an English graduate, however proletarian in origin'. If you want your book reproduced, he told an interviewer, 'go to television and ask for an eight-hour serial'.

Although published after *The Collector* (1963), *The Magus* was actually Fowles's first novel, to which he returned again and again during his long and gruelling literary apprenticeship. This began after he left Oxford in 1950, aged 24. He had arrived there as a clean young Englishman, whose pedigree included being head boy and captain of cricket at Bedford School, and holding a commission in the Royal Marines. At New College, which then had a reputation for intellectual rigour, he drew a line under his past, embracing existentialism and fancying himself a highbrow. Emerging with a Second in Modern Languages he turned down a job at Winchester College and chose instead to teach first at Poitiers University and then at a Greek boarding-school for boys on the tiny island of Spetsai. It was here that *The Magus* was conceived. And it was also here that he met Elizabeth Christy, who would become his wife.

A tall, striking blonde who has been identified as the model for Alison in *The Magus*, Elizabeth was married to a 'difficult' colleague of Fowles. The saga of her bitterly contested divorce is told in excruciating detail by Fowles's biographer Eileen Warburton. Uneducated, but acutely perceptive about Fowles's writing, Elizabeth described her editing duties as 'delousing'. Without her *The Magus* would probably have been stillborn.

Spetsai enchanted Fowles, the latest in a long line of English writers to succumb to the allure of the warm South. But it was the landscape rather than the ambience that beguiled him. One day, gazing out to sea from a sunny vantage point, he had an epiphany: 'Landscapes like this, on such days, advance men immeasurably. Perhaps ancient Greece was only the effect of a landscape and a light on a sensitive people.'

Newly arrived on Phraxos, the name Fowles gave to Spetsai,

Nicholas Urfe also invokes ancient Greece: 'There was something pleasantly absurd about teaching in a boarding-school (run on supposedly Eton-Harrow lines) only a look north from where Clytemnestra killed Agamemnon.' But what Nicholas feels most is 'emotional triumph' at having successfully ditched someone – Alison – who loved him more than he loved her: 'I had in some undefinable way won.' He knows this is 'odious' of him but is too excited at the prospect of 'taking wing' again to feel much remorse.

The novel's first fifty pages recreate this doomed affair. They meet at a bottle party in London's flatland – a trip down memory lane for me – and immediately go to bed. She is Australian, sexy, promiscuous, tough on the outside but emotionally fragile. He is a more raffish version of Fowles himself, a Brigadier's son with enough money of his own to run a car (Fowles never learnt to drive), a plausible manner and a strong sense of entitlement. Alison sees through him but can't help falling for him in a big way, so that when, later on, he rejects her, it's reasonable to assume that she might take an overdose.

When out walking on Phraxos Nicholas meets an elderly gent called Conchis, a cosmopolitan millionaire who owns a large secluded villa, full of priceless artefacts, on the other side of the island. Part impresario, part sorcerer, Conchis – 'The Magus' – has had an amazingly eventful life that includes surviving both the Western Front and a Nazi firing squad, two harrowing episodes in which Fowles's mastery of narrative is established beyond doubt. Conchis befriends Nicholas, convinces him that he has been 'chosen', and then involves him in the 'godgame', a series of disturbing and hallucinatory 'happenings'. Though increasingly suspicious of Conchis's motives – is he a voyeur, an old queer, or what? – Nicholas cannot resist the bait that is dangled before him, a beautiful and enigmatic young *princesse lointaine* called Lily, with whom he is soon besotted.

Like everything else connected with Conchis, Lily – whose real name is Julie, and who has a twin sister called June – is not what she seems. Whenever they meet Nicholas is torn between trying to seduce her and trying to unmask her. There is a lot of verbal sparring, interspersed with unconsummated erotic interludes that only serve to stoke Nicholas's frustration. He becomes increasingly paranoid and suspects that everyone on the island is secretly laughing at his predicament. The regular debriefings he has with Conchis reminded me of an aphorism Ferdinand Mount coined about his schooldays at Eton: 'How they see through you, the best schoolmasters, and how little the seeing through does to change you.' So it is that when Nicholas learns, in a letter from her flatmate, that Alison has indeed taken an overdose, any grief he feels soon evaporates at the thought of finally bedding Lily.

Nicholas achieves his aim but is then so thoroughly humiliated that he vows to expose his tormentors. Sacked from the school for punching one of his colleagues, he is mortified to discover, on his way home, that Alison is alive, and must therefore have been complicit in almost everything he has suffered. Which is where we shall leave him for the moment.

In 1977 I interviewed Fowles at the small Hampstead flat he kept for his rare visits to London from Lyme Regis. Earlier in the year he had earned $500,000 in a single week from the advance for his fourth novel, *Daniel Martin*, and the film rights to *The French Lieutenant's Woman*. Why, I remember thinking, hadn't he spent some of it on his teeth, which looked mildewed. But he insisted that money was not what motivated him, describing himself as a 'compulsive storyteller – a kind of victim, almost, in that I cannot *not* write'. Hence the masses of unpublished – and unpublishable – material he'd accumulated since leaving Oxford.

Speaking in a soft voice that belied his burly frame, Fowles said his 'retarded' adolescence was the result of an institutional straitjacket: first boarding-school in wartime, then the Royal Marines. At Oxford his attempt to grow up and enjoy himself was hampered by chronic amoebic dysentery, so that by the time he came down he had a lot of ground to make up. Recalling the success of *The Magus*, which he pronounced with a short 'a', he said it seemed to have 'put people's critical faculties to sleep'. He'd received more letters about it than all his other books put together, 'very remarkable letters, some of them, from people who identified with the narrator, or who claimed to have had similar experiences'. He thought the fact that it was 'unashamedly narrative' helped to explain its appeal, also its 'fairy tale' element, which you didn't find in adult fiction.

Reviewing the revised version, an American critic said that 'whatever one's opinion of *The Magus*, no one ever wished it any longer, except John Fowles' – who had added another seventy pages. I agree. Fifty years on I was in danger of nodding off over the indulgent descriptions of flora and fauna – what my friend Simon Raven, who'd relished *The Collector*, called 'all those bloody pines on Greek islands'. And I grew impatient at the game-playing between Nicholas and Lily/Julie: 'For Christ's sake, get on with it!' Nor are there any laughs. Wit was one gift the Good Fiction Fairy withheld at Fowles's christening.

But just when you're ready to toss the book aside, Fowles, like Conchis, starts weaving his web again and you're compelled to read on. For instance, Conchis describes how, at the Battle of Neuve Chapelle in 1915, he spent a night in a shell hole full of decomposing corpses. He chooses a singular way of conveying to Nicholas what this was like. No pyrotechnics, just a faint chorus of 'Tipperary' and a nauseating cesspool stench that makes Nicholas want to throw up. Had Fowles, I wonder, read Sir William Orpen's memoirs, in which, recalling his stint as a war artist, he quotes an officer saying that while it would be possible to paint the Somme from memory, 'you couldn't paint the smell'? This of course is what's missing from all those elaborate trench systems you find at places like the Imperial War Museum.

Back in England Nicholas impatiently follows the trail that eventually leads back to Alison. En route he meets the twins' mother, an autumnal beauty and long-term lover of Conchis, who responds to his recriminations with a serenity that only increases his frustration. At one point she gives him a valuable ceramic plate. 'I think you should get used to handling fragile objects,' she says. And what then? Will Alison forgive him? Does he *deserve* to be forgiven?

Fowles said he'd rewritten the ending to make it less ambiguous, but I know I'm not alone in disputing this. It's still unclear whether they walk off together into the sunset or never see each other again. So the object of the exercise, to settle that argument I'd had, was in vain. But all was not lost, because a second reading revealed something that in my impetuous youth I'd missed, the importance to us all of Chance or, as Conchis calls it, Hazard. When you're young you believe you're master of your fate. When you're old, you raise a glass to Time and Chance and thank your lucky stars.

MICHAEL BARBER's son was conceived on a Greek island. He wonders if this was down to Hazard.

Dem Bones

PAULINE MELVILLE

Some thirty years ago in the National Museum of Guyana, amidst the geological, archaeological and historical artefacts in their display cabinets, there existed a carefully cordoned-off empty space. It consisted of a plinth covered in plush red fabric surrounded by gold tasselled ropes, as if waiting for secret royalty. I am not sure how many other countries set aside a space in their national museums for their ghosts, spirits and jumbies. Not many, I imagine. Behind the empty space hung various plaques with detailed sociological descriptions of each spirit, itemizing its habitat, appearance, customary behaviour and even dietary preferences, an attempt by the rational with its orderly classifications and categorizations to contain or overpower these disturbing beings.

Take Moon-Gazer for example. Moon-Gazer is about sixty feet tall and can be seen straddling roads on moonlit nights. It is clothed in white, and grows and diminishes as the moon rises and sets. It devours people who attempt to pass between its feet unless they are smoking a cigarette and remain silent. It harms people when the moon is hidden by clouds. And what about the Bush Dai-Dai? It has hairless yellow skin and is slightly shorter than a normal human being. It lives in the interior, has a tail but no knees and a reversed foot. People say it can be of either sex and that it guards Amerindian treasures. When annoyed it eats people or tears them to pieces. Favourite food, bananas.

Edgar Mittelholzer, *My Bones and My Flute* (1955)
Peepal Tree Press · Pb · 96pp · £9.99 · ISBN 9781845232955

In recent years the space in the museum has become less prominent and the gold tasselled ropes have gone. Rationalism has gained the upper hand.

I was reminded of all this recently when I picked up a novel by Edgar Mittelholzer, the Guyanese writer who first brought Guyana's fiction to the attention of Britain. The book is called *My Bones and My Flute* (1955), and on rereading it I was as terrified as I had been when I originally came across it in my youth. It is set in Berbice and concerns a spirit called the Dutchman.

Mittelholzer came from what was known then as a coloured family in the small town of New Amsterdam in the county of Berbice, originally a Dutch colony. When I last went there the only way to cross the Berbice River was by ferry although I believe there is now a floating bridge. The river is one of three great rivers in Guyana. Once when a friend of mine was visiting I organized a trip for her on the Essequibo River. When she saw the river she asked if she would need a passport. The river was so wide it was not possible to see the bank on the far side. She thought she was leaving the country.

I was making a trip to New Amsterdam to visit friends. While the rusty ferry was being loaded I waited at the pierhead or *stelling* as it is known, from the Dutch. The river was flat and wide, the waters a milky caramel colour, the air warm and windless. On the far side it was just possible to see a low green fringe of bush. There was nothing to indicate human habitation except one church spire that rose out of the green strip.

Guyana is a hugely underpopulated country and wherever there is a small town or settlement it is impossible to ignore the impermanence of human life in that setting, surrounded as it is by a vast hinterland of uninhabited rainforest, bush, swamp, river and savannah. It affects Guyanese writers and in Mittelholzer's work characters can seem to have a closer contact with nature than with family or society. He paints pictures of 'the green doldrums' and 'the dark green menace', 'the perpetual hissing of the rain' and 'the chirruping of tree-frogs'.

These days, unlike, say, Joseph Conrad or Herman Melville, writers have less contact with the elements, less chance to consider the relative puniness of their own existence. That day as I waited to board the ferry I was aware of the endless calm patience of the river, lapping at the wooden support beams of the *stelling* as if it were waiting to reassert itself over the manmade impediment.

Soon the ferry was chugging through the water overloaded with goods, sacks of grain and agricultural machinery. Passengers crowded together on deck, shoving and jostling each other, leaning over the railing, studying the waterline and wondering if the shuddering boat would sink. The crossing took twenty minutes.

From the landing-stage, I walked into a town in full rigor mortis. Many of the once stately wooden houses were dilapidated, sagging a little, their timbers cracked by the sun, the white paint peeling. I looked for New Street. There is a notion that the history and geography of South America are both so extreme as to appear fictional or even magical to outsiders. The line between fiction and reality is blurred. In New Street the modest single-storey houses on stilts were set at a distance from each other but they too were in disrepair and looked as unstable as a house of cards.

It was hot and I needed a cool drink. I couldn't see any numbers on the houses so I stopped a passer-by: 'Excuse me, sir, which house is number sixteen?' The man paused for a moment and then replied, 'They all number sixteen in this street.' I felt I was in a dream, though later I discovered that the whole street was indeed 'Lot Sixteen'. Eventually, I found the right house.

Later that day, as I wandered around town, I was reminded of Mittelholzer's landscapes, the glittering black waters of Canje Creek and the Dutch names of old plantations: Oostermeer and De Hoop. In 1763 there was a great slave rebellion in Berbice: 2,500 slaves rose up against their Dutch colonial masters. Cuffy the leader declared himself governor of Berbice. The uprising was brutally put down by the Dutch commander van Hoogenheim. Many lives were lost. The

Dutchman's spirit is supposed to patrol the borders of plantations, sometimes on horseback.

The story of *My Bones and My Flute* is set in the 1930s. It concerns the Nevinsons, a New Amsterdam family, owners of a timber factory a hundred miles up-river in Goed de Vries. A canister discovered there contains an old parchment written in Dutch. Mr Nevinson decides to investigate. He takes his wife, daughter and a friend, all of whom have handled the parchment. It turns out that whoever touches the parchment begins to hear a flute playing and later becomes subject to an enormous force that drags them towards the river. One local Amerindian woman has already drowned with the mark of a flute branded on her thigh. The parchment was apparently written by a Dutch planter whose wife and children had been slaughtered in the uprising. He wrote in hiding, knowing he would die, demanding that his bones be given a Christian burial alongside his flute and cursing anyone who did not comply. He saw himself surrounded by spiritual forces that were evil and Satanic.

Mittelholzer was exceptionally well-read, and in *My Bones and My Flute* he produced a traditional ghost story to match those of Edgar Allan Poe and M. R. James. He recreates the oppressive atmosphere of the bush, the metallic call of a bird, the rank musky smell of a creek's rotting vegetation and the needle-fine whine of mosquitoes. What is happening inside the family house is contrasted with the everyday sound of the saw-mill engines, the workers' voices and daily life carrying on as usual somewhere not too far away.

Inside the house those dark spirits take on different manifestations: sometimes the figure of a man; sometimes a grey furry sub-human presence humping along the floor; a swirling mist that enters and sinks into the daughter; a goatish stench; the stigmata of a flute on the skin. They always have the same effect of dragging the victim towards the river to be drowned. The only thing that can keep them at bay is fire – a match, a candle, an oil lamp.

The function of the bone-flute in pre-Columbian and pre-

Christian Amerindian cultures is highly debatable. But there are stories of Macusi and Warao origin where the flute is particularly magical in dispelling evil spirits and making sure a certain area remains sacred. Who knows whether that idea was lodged somewhere in Mittelholzer's psyche? In his story, the flute is ambiguous. It could be either a good or a bad force, but eventually the family follows the sound deep into the bush. Anyone who wishes to know the rest of the story can read it for themselves.

After my wander around town I returned to the house where all the conversation was about the chloroform robbers who rendered their victims unconscious while they carried out their robberies. That was many years ago. I think New Amsterdam has had a facelift since then, and a friend confirmed it: 'Yes. Ah believe dem a nice it up now.'

In the village of Mahaica in Demerara, a ritual takes place every so often where a table is laid with delicious snacks and jellies and left out overnight to appease the spirits of the English dead in a cemetery nearby. I asked a woman why the same ceremony was not conducted for the Dutch, who also occupy part of the cemetery. In the sun her face shone with scorn. She replied: 'Everyone knows that the Dutch are unappeasable.'

Edgar Mittelholzer's work is out of fashion now. Sometimes his writing is lurid and populist, but it can also be powerful. His personal attitudes, his avowed racism and extreme right-wing opinions are judged to be abhorrent. For the last half of his life he relocated to the English home counties, Farnham to be precise, where he chose to commit suicide by pouring petrol on himself and setting himself alight.

I am writing this in England in May. In Guyana it is the rainy season and I think of the heavy rains falling endlessly over that vast uninhabited expanse of bush.

PAULINE MELVILLE's latest collection of short stories, *The Master of Chaos*, was published in 2021.

Guilty Pleasures

KEN HAIGH

More often than not, a shelf of books is a statement about the person we wish to be. We carefully arrange the titles so our friends will gain a favourable impression of us, thinking that we are cultured, sensitive, politically aware or part of the rebellious avant-garde. Meanwhile, the books we really enjoy, our guilty pleasures, are hidden from sight. It's nice to know that not much has changed in 500 years. Apparently, scholars in Ming-dynasty China did much the same. The books on display in their studies were the Confucian classics they had been forced to read to gain high positions in the civil service, while the books they really enjoyed were hidden under their mattresses. And these, quite often, were pulp detective novels.

Yes, the Chinese invented detective fiction. These stories began as folk tales told by itinerant storytellers in marketplaces or tea houses, lurid accounts of murder, lust and betrayal, whose heroes were cunning and incorruptible Tang- or Song-dynasty magistrates with names like Bao, Peng or Dee. Then, in the Ming dynasty (1368–1644), the tales were written down, often anonymously, and published in inexpensive editions for the literati to enjoy in private.

We might not know of these stories at all if it weren't for a scholarly Dutch diplomat named Robert van Gulik. When Japan declared war on the Netherlands in late 1941, van Gulik was forced to flee his

Robert van Gulik, *The Chinese Maze Murders* (1951)
University of Chicago Press · Pb · 336pp · £10 · ISBN 9780226848785
Many of van Gulik's other Judge Dee stories are also available in paperback from the University of Chicago Press.

embassy in Tokyo for Chungking, the wartime capital of China. He took with him a small, lithographed copy of an eighteenth-century Chinese crime novel, entitled *Four Important and Curious Cases in the Time of Empress Wu*, and, in moments stolen between his diplomatic duties and Japanese air raids, he read the novel for amusement. However, it wasn't until after the war, when he was posted to Washington and was exposed to American pulp detective novels, that he decided to translate the book into English.

When he was transferred back to Tokyo in 1948, van Gulik published his translation in a small privately printed edition as *Dee Goong An: Three Murder Cases Solved by Judge Dee*, noting in the afterword: 'It might be an interesting experiment if one of our modern writers of detective stories would try his hand at composing an ancient Chinese detective story himself.' His suggestion was directed at Chinese and Japanese authors who were then flooding the Asian markets with third-rate imitations of American crime novels. *Dee Goong An* was a modest success, and when no one took up the gauntlet, van Gulik decided to follow his own advice and create more Judge Dee stories.

He realized that he couldn't translate the stories just as he found them: he would have to adapt them to the tastes of a modern audience. Ancient Chinese detective stories usually begin by introducing the criminal and then follow the magistrate's progress in tracking them down, often with the help of supernatural agents or dreams rather than logic. These old books are also very long, with digressions on religious or philosophical matters, and they always end with a gruesome depiction of the criminal's execution. A modern audience would have no patience with all this so, taking plot lines from the Chinese originals, van Gulik began to write his own stories in the modern style. One thing he did keep, however, was the Chinese practice of having the magistrate solve several unrelated crimes at the same time. He felt this was a more realistic portrayal of a busy magistrate's life than the one-mystery-per-book tradition of modern Western detective fiction.

The first of these original novels was *The Chinese Maze Murders* (1951), published initially in Japanese and Chinese editions, and only later in English. But as it turned out it was the English-speaking world that really warmed to Judge Dee. So van Gulik's subsequent Judge Dee books – another fourteen novels, one collection of short stories and two novellas bound as one volume – were written primarily for the English-speaking market.

Judge Dee was a real person, a Tang-dynasty magistrate and statesman with a reputation for honesty and incorruptibility named Di Renjie, who lived from AD 630 to 700, but the stories ascribed to him are entirely fictitious. Van Gulik's Dee is a detective with a difference, for in the Chinese court system, a magistrate acted as judge, jury, prosecutor and detective. Dee is assisted by several lieutenants who follow him from post to post and so form a core of loyal and incorruptible assistants. In the original stories these figures were often petty criminals whom the judge had caught and reformed. In the case of Judge Dee, he is assisted by Sergeant Hoong, an old family retainer (a kind of Watson to Dee's Holmes); Tao Gan, a former confidence man; and Ma Joong and Chiao Tai, highway bandits Dee has recruited as muscle and who serve in the novels as comic relief. And though Di Renjie was a Tang-dynasty official, van Gulik's Judge Dee stories reflect the sixteenth-century world in which they were first written down.

Another reason for translating *Dee Goong An*, van Gulik explains in his introduction, was to reflect a more authentic view of Chinese life. Western readers had met Chinese detectives before in Earl D. Biggers's hero Charlie Chan and Chinese criminals in Sax Rohmer's Fu Manchu, but neither of these did justice to Chinese reality. The joy of reading the Judge Dee stories lies in their portrayal of Chinese society at the time. Indeed, Van Gulik did such a good job in portraying Chinese culture that, for a while, his novels were required reading for US Foreign Service officials posted to China.

If I had to pick a favourite, it would be *The Haunted Monastery*

(1961), in which Judge Dee and his family are storm-bound in a remote Daoist monastery, and Dee must solve multiple mysteries over the course of a single night. If you like your mysteries served with a touch of the gothic, this is the one for you. However, if you are new to the Judge Dee stories, you should probably start with *The Chinese Gold Murders* (1959), the first chronologically, in which the 33-year-old judge travels to his first appointment in Peng-lai, a small coastal town in north-east Shandong province. His challenge is to solve the murder of his predecessor in a classic locked-room puzzle, but he must also locate a runaway bride and discover why the corpse of a dead monk has been found in the grave of a murdered woman.

I am the first to admit that van Gulik is not a literary stylist, but I don't read him for his prose style. I read him because the stories are fun. So why, you might ask, are they not displayed proudly on my bookshelves at home? The answer is quite simple. The cover illustration on each of my old paperback editions almost invariably features a block-print image of a naked woman. At first glance, it looks as if I own a collection of antique Chinese pornography. Apparently, van Gulik's Japanese publisher thought these racy covers were a selling feature, so he insisted that van Gulik source old prints to use as illustrations, and where he couldn't find suitable prints, draw his own in the Chinese style. In the process, van Gulik became quite an expert on Chinese erotica; he even published a scholarly book on the subject. Fortunately for you, dear reader, the modern reprints have dispensed with the old cover illustrations and replaced them with family-friendly images – ones you wouldn't be ashamed to display to your friends.

Having recently retired as the director of a public library in Canada, KEN HAIGH had hoped to reward himself with a long journey to some foreign land. Instead, he spent the pandemic travelling vicariously in place and time through his reading. His most recent book is *On Foot to Canterbury*.

Read, then Cook

OLIVIA POTTS

'If you can read, you can cook.' This was the simple, revolutionary philosophy behind *Mastering the Art of French Cooking* (1961 and 1970), written by Julia Child, Simone Beck and Louisette Bertholle. Even with sixty years' hindsight, the book's lasting success is remarkable. In two volumes and running to well over a thousand pages of precise technical French cuisine it was launched on a nation of home cooks who knew little about *la belle France,* yet it became a runaway best-seller and catapulted one of its authors to fame.

The first volume was published in 1961, at a time when women were leaving the home and finding employment, when domestic technology was booming, when convenience was king. One unenthusiastic publisher dismissed the project, saying: 'Americans don't want an encyclopedia, they want to cook something quick, with a mix.' They would soon be decisively proved wrong.

Beck and Bertholle, both Frenchwomen, had already written a cookbook when they met Child: a wide-ranging book of French recipes for American cooks. It had been taken on by a publisher who had had it translated and named it *What's Cooking in France?* It turned out to be an embarrassment: it was inadequately translated, poorly put together and badly received. Chagrined and disappointed, they turned to their new American friend Julia Child in the hope that

Julia Child, Louisette Bertholle & Simone Beck, *Mastering the Art of French Cooking*, Vol. 1 (1961) · Penguin · Pb · 784pp · £12.99 · ISBN 9780241956465; Julia Child & Simone Beck, *Mastering the Art of French Cooking*, Vol. 2 (1970) · Penguin · Pb · 688pp · £12.99 · ISBN 9780241956472.

she would help them salvage the book and republish it. After looking at what had been produced and testing some of the recipes, she insisted they start from scratch. So that's what they did. From the moment of Child's involvement, she became the driving force behind what would become *Mastering the Art of French Cooking*.

Julia Child (née McWilliams) was born in 1912 in Pasadena, California to wealthy parents: her father was a successful landowner and developer. She was expensively educated at a boarding-school in Marin County and then, following in her mother's footsteps, enrolled in Smith College, where she majored in history. Her enrolment form asked what vocation she had in mind. Child wrote, 'No occupation decided; Marriage preferable.' After college, she spent time in New York working as a copywriter, then returned to Pasadena. She was restless. In 1942, she joined the Office of Strategic Services and a couple of years later was posted to Kandy in Ceylon, where she met Paul Child. Paul and Julia married in 1946, and two years later they moved to Paris for Paul's work.

It was there that Julia Child truly fell in love with food. She had grown up with a full-time cook and had no experience of cooking. Eating out in Paris was an unadulterated joy for her, and she quickly became obsessed with French food, but her culinary attempts at home were hit-and-miss. While she was looking for something to occupy her days, her husband came home with the address of Le Cordon Bleu. She joined a course there but found it too simplistic and her classmates too frivolous; she quickly managed to get herself transferred to the institution's professional cookery course. Learning to cook French cuisine extended her passion from French flavour to French technique.

After her exams, a friend introduced her to fellow food enthusiast Simone Beck. Simca, as Julia would come to call her, had grown up in Normandy, and had the culinary intuition and inheritance which proved to be the perfect match for Julia's practice-makes-perfect attitude. The two women formed a close friendship that lasted for the rest of their lives.

From the get-go, Child had high hopes for what would become *Mastering the Art of French Cooking*. She told her lawyer – who had the temerity to suggest that *any* publishing deal was a good deal for an unknown author – 'I see no reason to crawl about on our stomachs. This is no amateur affair written by little women who just love to cook, but a professional job written by professionals; and, I would say without modesty, even a "major work" on the principles of French Cooking. I therefore have no intention of wasting it on a no-account firm.'

Bertholle, Beck and Child were all trained by Le Cordon Bleu in Paris, but the point of their book was that it was for people who lacked any formal training. Child had a different perspective on cooking to that of Beck and Bertholle: she had come to French cookery as an adult, and had learnt deliberately, rather than instinctively. This informed everything she did. 'Cooking is one failure after another, and that's how you finally learn,' she later told her TV audience. She was adamant that every recipe in the book must be developed and tested to the point of it being foolproof.

The first volume took six years to research and write, contained 524 recipes and ran to over 700 pages of soups, sauces, eggs, entrées and luncheon dishes, fish, poultry, meat, vegetables, cold buffet, desserts and cake. It covered everything from a simple leek and potato soup to how to use veal knuckles for jellied stock.
It taught you how to cook soufflés and sweetbreads, and how to debone a duck and why you might need to do so. There were already many books and magazines on French cooking available for American readers, but all of them assumed considerable knowledge of French culinary technique. Child wanted to

create something different: a book that would take a novice from béchamel sauce to a foolproof *Pâté de canard en croûte*.

It was this level of sometimes tedious precision that caused Bertholle to lose interest in the project. Child and Beck, in turn, became doubtful as to how much Bertholle was contributing, and whether she really deserved to be a co-author. Ultimately, she was given equal billing for the first volume, but a lower royalty. Unsurprisingly, this caused a rift between the three women, and she was not involved in the second volume.

Julia Child was an outsider in the world of French food. She hadn't grown up cooking; she was an expat who had arrived in France through marriage and accident, rather than under her own steam. Even physically, she stood out: she was six foot two, and possessed a distinctive, warbling voice. She was 41 when she enrolled in Le Cordon Bleu, and 42 when she began writing recipes. But all of this meant she was uniquely able to understand what someone who knew nothing about French food needed to know in order to cook it.

Like Child, I came to cookery late, without knowledge or instinct; with enthusiasm but no confidence. Like Child, I went to Le Cordon Bleu, and when I did, it was reassuring to know that a tall, loud and bumbling woman had found her feet there. When I read *Mastering the Art of French Cooking*, I greatly appreciated her diligent handholding, which didn't assume instinct or culinary common sense, because, frankly, I had none. Ultimately, Julia Child helped me become a much better cook.

Child had no time for those who preferred to wrap French cooking up in pomp and mystery. She once wrote to her long-time pen pal Avis DeVoto: 'They were talking about Beurre Blanc, and how it was a mystery, and only a few people could do it, and how it could only be made with white shallots from Lorraine over a *wood fire*. Phoo. But that is so damned typical, making a damned mystery out of perfectly simple things just to puff themselves up.' She expanded on the theme in her introduction to *Mastering the Art of French Cooking*'s first volume:

> We have purposely omitted cobwebbed bottles, the *patron* in his white cap bustling among his sauces, anecdotes about charming little restaurants with gleaming napery, and so forth. Such romantic interludes, it seems to us, put French cooking into a 'never-never' land instead of the Here, where happily it is available to everybody. Anyone can cook in the French manner anywhere, with the right instruction.

It is for this reason that, unlike most of the food writing I'm drawn to, *Mastering the Art of French Cooking* doesn't include any personal or historical narrative. No charming stories lurk between the recipes. It is purely an instructional manual. It's interesting to contrast Julia Child with her British contemporary Elizabeth David, who all but single-handedly brought Mediterranean cooking to British shores. In *French Provincial Cooking*, in the introduction to the hors d'oeuvres section, David dedicates several pages to a particular café she visited in Remoulins when filling her car with petrol. Child simply states, 'For those who enjoy making pastries, here are a few good hot hors d'oeuvres and one cold one,' before launching into a recipe for Roquefort cheese balls.

Despite various publishing hiccups and the occasional waning in enthusiasm, Beck and Child never lost faith in the belief that there would be an audience for their book. Their faith was justified: within five years of publication the first volume had sold 100,000 copies, despite little publicity. Both volumes have since been reprinted many times, and they became the basis for a very successful film, *Julie and Julia* (2009). *Mastering the Art of French Cooking* launched Child on a television career that would last the rest of her life and turn her into a household name.

In one sense, the book was very much of its time: it opens with the line 'This is a book for the servantless cook.' It arrived during a period when many households had given up domestic help, and women (mostly) who had never cooked before were entering the kitchen for the first time. But in another way, the book was and remains timeless: its comprehensive nature meant that for the following sixty years, it became a first port of call for anyone interested in French cuisine, and I believe it still is.

Julia Child died in 2004 at the age of 91. It is perhaps ironic, given her early lack of ambition, that she would go on to spearhead a book that was unprecedented in scope and ambition. Child was a woman who found her passion later in life, who began cooking at 41, who had her first book published at 49, and who then became a national treasure. Once she'd found cookery and writing – giving others confidence through the medium of her recipes – she was unstoppable. But her professional steeliness was matched by her unwavering belief that cooking was not only available to anyone willing to give it a go, but also a potential source of joy. As she says in the first volume of *Mastering the Art of French Cooking*, 'Above all, have a good time.'

OLIVIA POTTS is a food writer and chef. Her first book, *A Half Baked Idea*, won the Fortnum & Mason debut food book award, and her second book, *Butter: A Celebration*, will be published this September. You can also hear her on our podcast, Episode 23, 'A Writer in the Kitchen'.

Lark, Hare, Stone

ROBIN BLAKE

Memories of the British Empire may be receding around the world, but they live on in Ireland, the first and closest of Britain's colonies. It is not hard to see why. For centuries all the techniques that would eventually be deployed to subdue various other peoples were initiated there: armed force, mass slaughter, the theft of land, economic and racial bullying, the suppression of language, enslavement, starvation. Then, as they cut their losses, the British played their final card – partition.

The north-south Irish border has just had its centenary, around which there were many reminders of how it has been variously imagined. Yes, it's a line on the map. But it may also be, as the late John Hume said, a boundary across the mind, not to mention a gash, a gouge, a serpent in the road, a deadly trap, a razor's edge. For two recent decades, between the Good Friday Agreement of 1998 and its Brexit nemesis, the border was reconfigured as a bridge between sectarian opponents. Seamus Heaney had a typically down-to-earth alternative image: a man carrying two buckets.

But post-Brexit the border is once again a squiggly 310-mile-long frontier between either and or: in or out, cheap or expensive, Catholic or Protestant. On the ground it falls across field, mountain, lake and river. To write well about it therefore means to be as committed to

Shane Connaughton, *A Border Station* (1989) · Black Swan · Pb · 240pp · £8.99 · ISBN 9781784162559; *The Run of the Country* (1991) is out of print; *Married Quarters* (2017) · Black Swan · Pb · 336pp · £9.99 · ISBN 9781784162566 the land itself as to the people who live there. I know of no writing set in the Irish border lands where this double commitment is stronger – by turns comic, pastoral, lyrical, tragic – than in Shane Connaughton's three books about them, *A Border Station* (1989), *The Run of the Country* (1991) and *Married Quarters* (2017).

Lady Mabel Annesley, 'Landscape with Houses', wood engraving

As a native of the Cavan-Monaghan region, where republican land bulges into the northern county of Fermanagh, Connaughton knows exactly how this 'drunken geography' uproots political theory. 'The land was impervious to maps. What appeared plain on paper was on the ground an orgy of political and geographical confusion, Cavan and Monaghan in the South were locked into Fermanagh in the North like two dogs trying to cover the one hot bitch.' The simile shouldn't really work, but Connaughton can make you understand how the soil and geology of the place move in time with the plants and creatures alive in them: the whins on the hillside, the wheat in the fields, the starlings in the air, the rats in the midden, the cows in the shed. In *The Run of the Country* he goes back repeatedly to a triple image – lark, hare, stone – a trinity to represent the delight, the fear and the obduracy of life on the border.

This novel and two collections of stories, *A Border Station* and *Married Quarters*, together chronicle the life of an unnamed boy growing up during the 1950s in the fictional village of Butlershill, standing just within the republican side of the border. There is always the danger of stereotyping in writing about Ireland, and this place is indeed built on blocks familiar from rural life across the country: farming, religion, drink, debt, repressed sex and impractical dreams, to which are added the more localized border activities of smuggling and blowing up customs posts. But in Connaughton's hands these combine to give a powerful sense of life both microscopically local and cinemascopically universal. Connaughton is an Oscar-winning screenwriter, and both structurally and thematically he knows what he's doing.

Butlershill, as shown in the tales of *A Border Station* and *Married Quarters*, bursts with all the self-importance of a small world. The boy's big-fisted, permanently angry father is the Sergeant at its *garda siochana* barracks (the police station), and as such one of the two local pillars of authority. The other is Father Gaynor, a priest who thinks as little of his bishop as the Sergeant does of his own superiors. One reason for the Sergeant's frustration is that he has been relegated to this forgotten corner of the border for political reasons and must fritter his time away on 'farmers who allowed donkeys to walk the roads unshod, bicycles with no rear lights and neighbours fighting over trespassing cattle'. His rage against this fate has all the anguish of Job on his dunghill. 'Donkeys and bicycle pumps! Me! Who worked on three murder cases in me day. One good murder, that's all I ask. One good murder!'

The Sergeant, in his great heavily welted boots, is in every sense a massive presence in the books. Looming less large, but looming nevertheless, are many other salty characters in the boy's world. These include Tully, the shifty publican-cum-grocer, the organ-playing farmer Conlon, whose music maddens the bull in the field above, the severe but sexy Methodist Tilly Roberts preaching to the hated Papists because 'if she couldn't save them she would annoy them', and the rapacious smuggler Rinty, whose corrugated-iron emporium sited on the edge of a field will furnish his customers with anything from ladies' knickers to a set of tractor tyres.

There are also two precarious remnants of the Anglo-Irish ascendancy. One is the crumbling big house and demesne of Lady Sarah Butler-Coote, ancient and moribund survivor of her line. The other is Castle Finn, perched above the river border, the Finn itself, where handsome but feckless Colonel Bridge and his American heiress wife Sophie Kay drink around the clock while their money dribbles away. Both are left stranded on the wrong side of the frontier, in what is still known around there as the Free State. The local Catholics, all deference gone, regard them with tolerance combined with (in Lady Sarah's case) affection and (in the Colonel's) contempt.

But more important in the boy's eyes than any of these supporting characters, though in exact equilibrium with his rampaging father, is the counterweight of his mother ('the mystery of his mother was her gentleness'). She gives him the outlet for his feelings of uncertainty and tenderness, but this is stopped quite shockingly with her death near the beginning of *The Run of the Country*. Before that moment childhood still lingered, and fear and pleasure were evenly balanced. Afterwards he is sent skittering towards adulthood, with all its new desires and agonies, its comedies and tragedies.

Connaughton's two short-story collections are arresting portraits of the artist as a young Mammy's boy, but the novel is his masterpiece. The boy is now 17, a bookish virginal school-leaver who, with his mother dead, finds it impossible to live any longer at the barracks. He takes refuge at the farm of his friend and mentor, the 19-year-old Prunty, who leads him in a gallivant around the country that takes in a visit to the horse-knacker's yard, a tense smuggling trip, a punch-up with Protestants at a local hop, the committing of sacrilege in Father Gaynor's sacristy, and a cockfight in a distant field. Prunty is Mercutio to the boy's Romeo, fearless, voluble ('The language shot out of Prunty's mouth rough and rich as a forkful of dung') and always skirting the edges of danger. The Shakespearean analogy is just, because halfway into the plot *The Run of the Country* turns into a Romeo and Juliet love story with the appearance in the boy's life of Annagh Lee. Named after a river (and evidently akin to Joyce's Anna Livia Plurabelle) she is beautiful, but she lives across the border in the North and comes from an aggressively Protestant tribe. Their love is instinctive, lyrical, passionate and sexual (though happily this side of candidacy for the Bad Sex Award), but it trails tragedy behind it, along with disgrace and a final degrading punishment.

In the year of *The Run of the Country*'s publication, its reviewer in the *Times Literary Supplement* made a schoolmarmish comment on Connaughton's style: 'Over-writing is a temptation for this author.' I take over-writing to be the raising of language to flowery heights that are inappropriate to its immediate needs. But Connaughton's poetic prose, it seems to me, is exactly what is needed here. Sensibility at 17 really is heady, moonshiny, adjectival and poetic, and Connaughton's lyricism is true to that. In fact, it often reads like poetry from the school of Heaney. At one point 'from a blackthorn bush a blackbird rifled out and away, a panic of glassy notes breaking from its orange beak'. At another the boy surprises a hare which 'blurred to speed, disappearing in a necklace of spurting leaps', and again, lying in a wet ditch to escape the customs men, he notices how 'from the clayey bank a flute of water whispered over a tuft of watercress'.

Occasionally the language is bathetic, as when 'the moon melting into the Ulster Canal spread through the water like toasted cheese'. More often it is curt, visceral and cuts into the pith of life, as when the boy sees his father butcher a chicken or the knacker destroy a horse, or when Prunty's bruised face after the dancehall fight looks 'as if his assailant had left a knuckle under the skin'.

And it's hard, for me at least, to resist writing so well seasoned with dialect words – gauson, gulpin, scaldy, ojus, a widdy woman, a clocken hen, cracked milk, crigging your toes.

These books were written after the start of the Troubles, about a time before them. The upsurge in the 1970s of sectarian violence, and our image of it, scarred the border areas – Omagh, Crossmaglen, Armagh – with Armalite attacks and Semtex explosions, tear-gas canisters and rubber bullets. The images we retain of this are grey and gritty, so to read Connaughton is to remember that there is an older, more coloured truth pre-dating those images. The border was already there of course, and the gunfire and explosions were there too, but in these books the violence is still occasional and feels more like background music, or a matter of form, than terrorism. The real terror here is in everyday deeds and words, and particularly words spoken in anger. 'It was worth dying for, the last word,' says Connaughton when the boy's parents argue. 'Words were swords. A sentence was for life.'

For the people in these books, how the border affects their daily lives is what counts. Poverty, social envy, a pregnancy conceived with someone of the wrong religion, even the mortal Catholic sin of attending a Protestant funeral, all have evil consequences. And meanwhile, in counterpoint, nature takes its own sweet path.

As a writer Connaughton, like Heaney, is carrying a couple of buckets, but the point is not just the balance of the two, but what is inside them. In one the milk is certainly cracked and ojus, but the other is full of the freshest and creamiest buttermilk.

ROBIN BLAKE used to spend his summer holidays with his grandparents in Ireland, almost as far from the border as you can go. He is the author of eight mystery novels about the eighteenth-century coroner Titus Cragg and his friend Dr Luke Fidelis.

A Tale of Two Villages

WILLIAM PALMER

For many people in the countryside, life just after the Second World War had not changed so very much from a hundred years before. When I was a young boy in the 1950s our family lived in a small farmhouse in mid-Wales, a couple of miles from the nearest village. We had no mains water or electricity; water came from a well through a hand pump in the kitchen; electricity was provided by a generator – when that burned out one night in November we relied on candles and oil lamps for the whole winter. There was no bathroom, only a tin bath hung on the kitchen door, and an outside privy. Neighbouring farms were much the same, and families scratched a living from the sheep dotted on the surrounding hills. The children spoke Welsh and English and sang Welsh songs on the school bus. Most people went to Chapel on Sunday. It all seemed perfectly normal and likely to last forever.

But the writer Norman Lewis, returning to London in 1946 after three years on active service in North Africa and Italy, wrote that he 'looked for the familiar in England, but found change . . . it was the search for vanished times that drew me back to Spain'. This is from the foreword to *Voices of the Old Sea*, the account Lewis wrote of Farol, 'the least accessible coastal village in north-east Spain'. You will look in vain for Farol on any map: Lewis made the name up. It doesn't matter: for him the real place had long ceased to exist by the time his book came to be published in 1984.

Norman Lewis, *Voices of the Old Sea* (1984)
Eland · Pb · 208pp · £12.99 · ISBN 9781906011611

Like most of his writing, *Voices* is a warning against corruption – he had already written about the distortion of moral and political life by the Mafia in Sicily and later targets included the destruction of ancient cultures by American evangelical missionaries in South America, and the industrialization of rural India. At first, in 1948, he thought he had found in Farol what he had always searched for: an untouched and ancient society.

When Lewis arrived he lodged in the village inn, 'generally agreed to be the worst in Spain'. He was driven out by the smell of cats. The village was overrun with them, 'an ugly breed, skinny with long legs, and small pointed heads. You saw little of them in the daytime, but after dark they were everywhere.'

He moved quarters to lodge with a formidable woman known to everyone as Grandmother. 'Large, dignified and slow-moving', she dominated the lives of the women of Farol, prescribing herbal remedies, providing advice on birth control (condoms were illegally supplied by the local clairvoyant), giving permission for when it was proper for a couple to have a child, and even naming their children. The names were taken from a book on great generals, so the village was full of 'inoffensive little boys called Julio César, Carlo Magna and Napoleon'. Her daughter and son-in-law, Sebastian, lived with Grandmother in a state of some friction over Sebastian's seeming unwillingness, or inability, to produce a grandchild.

Farol had fifty houses, a small, decayed church, a ship's chandler's, a butcher's shop and a general store selling a wide range of goods 'from moustache wax to hard black chocolate that had to be broken up with a hammer'. There was also a bar, used by the local fishermen and called The Mermaid for its display of 'the mummified corpse of a dugong' hanging from the ceiling. The fishermen gathered under the 'mermaid' every evening. Their usual language was Catalan, but to tell tales of their days at sea they used classic Castilian in a form of rhythmic verse that was an extraordinary mixture of the everyday and the Homeric. If a stranger entered and took too much notice, they reverted to gossip in the local Catalan dialect. Lewis was schooled by Sebastian to make himself modestly retiring in the bar, so that the often very beautiful incantations could continue, and he finally felt accepted by Farol when he heard his own name pop up only half satirically in a fishing yarn.

The local church was neglected, as custom prevented any male from attending Mass, and the unmanly piety of the nearby village of Sort was ridiculed. Fortunately, Farol's priest Don Ignacio, whose main interest was in digging up whatever small artefacts he could find in nearby Roman ruins, was an easy-going, lovable and comic figure, as was his friend, Don Alberto, the aristocratic, quixotic local landowner. The two men had much in common:

> Don Ignacio's house was bare and claustrophobic as Don Alberto's, and he lived uncomfortably attended by an old woman virtually interchangeable from the one who looked after the old landowner . . . This grey-haired slatternly old creature was generally accepted – as in the case of Don Alberto's housekeeper – to have been his mistress . . .

This, in an irreligious village, gave a little prestige to the genial priest. And his friend Don Alberto was a charitable and generous landlord to his tenants, though not a rich man by any means. The two were the only educated men for miles around, scholars who loved to discuss local customs and traditions, to regret the passing of some and to laud the staying power of others. All in all, for them, and for Lewis, the two villages, Farol and Sort, had remained unchanged in their customs and essentials of life for centuries, partly because of their physical isolation at the end of a precipitous dirt road that was often impassable in winter.

It is easy to sympathize with Lewis's respect for the tough, independent, bloody-minded fishermen and the eccentricities of the impoverished landowner and priest. He became a fisherman himself in partnership with his friend Sebastian, and the lovingly detailed descriptions of diving and fishing in crystal waters are superb. The two men maintained a safe distance from the professionals, diving only for those fish that the Farol men ignored.

But any illusion that the people in these isolated villages lived an idyllic life, playing guitars and feasting on Elizabeth David dishes, is dispelled by this book. The guitar was despised, the meals were mostly stews of poor meat, and the wine was thin and acidic. Between October and March, hunkering down for the long winter, the fishermen had to live on the proceeds from their summer catch. Lewis may have made great efforts to fit in and he certainly helped many of the hopelessly innumerate locals order their affairs and avoid being cheated by the French dealers who came down to buy their fish, but he doesn't seem to have hung around much when summer ended.

Perhaps his unsullied vision could have lasted a little longer, but change came suddenly. Disaster and rescue, of a sort, arrived in three forms: a great storm, a virus and Jaime Muga.

A poor fishing season was succeeded by an October storm that left three of the five largest fishing boats smashed to pieces on the beach. The neighbours and rivals in Sort were also suffering. The forest of evergreen oaks from which cork was traditionally harvested was greying and dying, infested by a virus. The long-term existence of the two villages was in doubt as the young began to move away to look for work in the cities.

And Muga? He was a local black marketeer who set out to save Farol and Sort from themselves – and for himself. Lewis noticed the first changes when he returned for his second summer. The local inn bore a new sign: 'Guests admitted. Salubrious accommodation, and meals served at all hours.' Builders had ripped out the labyrinth of odd-shaped rooms and replaced them with fourteen bedrooms. 'Three bathrooms were incorporated, an exotic extravagance in local eyes.' The first guests arrived at the end of May, 'providing instant and final confirmation that all outsiders were basically irrational, when not actually mad'.

Muga's grip on the village rapidly grew stronger. He persuaded the younger fishermen to provide boat trips for the tourists and he cleaned up the waterfront. Three more hotels were quickly built. The general shop now sold tourist trash, and a new café served frozen hake brought up from Barcelona.

By the time Lewis came back for his third and last season, the old bar had been redecorated, the 'mermaid' had disappeared and the poetry had gone, replaced by ersatz flamenco music. His friend Sebastian had abandoned fishing; Lewis found him working, rather shamefaced, behind the desk at one of the hotels. There were many tourists now and some of the better-looking young fishermen earned handsome tips by sleeping with women tourists. The cats had been hunted down and killed. In three years, the ancient life of Farol had been destroyed and replaced by a tourist economy, while Sort had become a ghost town.

A few things had not changed: Lewis called on the priest Don Ignacio who, as usual, was entertaining his good friend Don Alberto. Talking of one of the few remaining fishermen who continued to hold to the belief that the tourists would depart and the good old days return, Don Ignacio said, 'Sometimes it is necessary to believe things that are absurd. When an illusion dies, a hope is born. He has as much right to his hope as we to our resignation.'

But Muga won. Welcome to the Costa Brava.

And our old cottage in Wales? We moved away in the '60s. A little while ago I found it on the Internet advertised as a 'self-catering holiday facility', with all mod cons.

WILLIAM PALMER's study of the place of alcohol in the lives and work of writers, *In Love with Hell*, was published in 2021 by Little, Brown. You can also hear him on our podcast, Episode 38, 'Literary Drinking'.

Murder, Miracles and Myanmar

ALASTAIR GLEGG

As I had expected, I found the famous murder trials edited by Miss F. Tennyson Jesse on the shelves of the Law Library of the University of Victoria on Vancouver Island, but I was pleasantly surprised to discover a dozen more of her books in the main collection. It is a very young university – a mere sixty years old – and it replaced Victoria College, which itself had absorbed the Normal School, as the teacher training institute was originally known, and naturally took over their libraries. Presumably the young women preparing to be junior school teachers in the 1920s and '30s enjoyed Jesse's novels and plays, and so obviously did their instructors and the librarians, who of course make the real decisions about library purchases.

It was through my interest in true crime that I first came across the work of Jesse – the F. was for 'Fryniwyd', a childhood Spoonerism of her real name, 'Wynifried', and 'Tennyson' was borrowed from her great-aunt – but only recently did I discover how much else she had written. In addition to her early poems and short stories she produced ten novels, several plays, historical works and books on criminology, all meticulously researched, intelligently argued, beautifully written and punctuated with flashes of sly humour.

F. Tennyson Jesse's *A Pin to See the Peepshow* (1934) is available in paperback from the British Library (320pp · £9.99 · ISBN 9780712353595). *The Lacquer Lady* (1929) was reissued by Virago in 1979 but is now out of print, as are her other books.

As a young writer Jesse worked as a reporter for *The Times* and the *Daily Mail*, and during the First World War she was sent to the Belgian front as a war correspondent. In 1918 the Ministry of Information asked if she would go to France to report on women's role in the war, but she told them, 'rather ungraciously, that if they wanted the "sunny-haired lassies-in-khaki touch" they had better send somebody else'. They agreed to her terms, and her objective yet sympathetic account, *The Sword of Deborah*, was published in 1919.

In 1924 Jesse wrote *Murder and Its Motives* in which she identified six reasons for the ultimate crime: Gain, Revenge, Elimination, Jealousy, Lust for Killing and Conviction (political or otherwise). She used some classic English examples but also included two notorious French cases: her knowledge of the language from her schooling in Paris allowed her to use sources beyond the reach of most other researchers. Her shrewd analyses and encyclopaedic knowledge of the field caught the attention of the criminologist Harry Hodge and led to an invitation to edit some of the *Notable British Trials* series: over the next thirty years she examined five famous murder cases, from the trial of Madeline Smith in 1857 to those of Evans and Christie ninety years later, the latter an account of a dreadful miscarriage of justice. She even took one celebrated case and turned it into a novel: although she claimed that 'every character in this book is entirely fictitious', *A Pin to See the Peepshow* (1934) is clearly based on the celebrated 1922 trial of Frederick Bywaters and Edith Thompson for the murder of her husband. As in the case of Madeline Smith, Edith's passionate letters to her lover played a crucial part in the case: should hints of future happiness together, if only her husband were out of the picture, be sufficient evidence of complicity in his murder?

Her 1937 novel *Act of God* is quite different and reminded me of the works of her more celebrated literary contemporary, Evelyn Waugh. It is set on the Riviera in a small unfashionable watering place with a population of locals and retired ladies and gentlemen of very limited means who do their best to maintain the appearance of a lifestyle they could not afford elsewhere. In the English Sporting Club 'women, too old to cash in on their looks, and too poor to be courted for their money, exploited their personalities as much as possible, chiefly by being intensely rude'.

Some years previously the town had been transformed: at a spring on a local hilltop 'no less a person than the Mother of God had appeared to two shepherd children'. The local curé believed their story, the bishop's various committees cautiously followed suit, and the apparition was officially recognized by the Church, but 'it is a dangerous thing to let a miracle loose upon the world'. Pilgrims flocked to be cured by the supposedly healing waters, some successfully, and tourists followed. Shops were soon crammed with 'the tawdry rubbish that it seems the peculiar genius of the Catholic religion and of seaside towns to collect', the locals became wealthy, and everything changed. Then one of the English residents discovered that the original 'miraculous' appearance was a hoax. The dilemma confronting those within and without the Church who become aware of the fraud is obvious, and goes back at least as far as Pontius Pilate's famous challenge: *'Quid est veritas?'* It is this question and its difficult answers that Jesse's characters explore in her story.

Her most ambitious novel, however, was *The Lacquer Lady*, set in Upper Burma in the 1880s and based on the research she carried out during two trips to Burma and interviews with local historians and several of the leading characters. They combine to produce a fascinating account which is really more fact than fiction. The underlying metaphor is the *tamein*, the silken skirt worn by Burmese women: not just the garment itself with its traditional and ceremonial importance, but the ritualistic weaving of the fabric which symbolizes the eternal but ever-changing pattern of life in the Golden Palace of Mandalay.

Fanny Moroni, the pretty but self-centered teenage daughter of an Italian father and an Anglo-Burmese mother, is attending boarding-school in Victorian England. Her father is a weaver (a prestigious occupation at the Palace in Mandalay) who had fallen out of favour but has now been reinstated. On finishing school Fanny returns to Burma but she finds the narrow European social round tedious compared to the glamour and luxury of the Golden Palace with its pomp and rituals. She cultivates a friendship with Supaya-lat, the young and ruthlessly ambitious princess whose reputation became notorious, familiar even to Rudyard Kipling's British soldier, who fondly remembers kissing a girl of the same name in his poem 'Mandalay'.

In Burma there is no right of primogeniture for royal succession: as the old king Mindoon is dying Princess Supaya-lat conspires to become queen and seduces one of his sons, who is named as the king's successor. Fanny becomes the new queen's 'spoilt pet' and is appointed a Maid of Honour. At the time Britain is suffering military setbacks in South Africa and the Sudan, which emboldens the new king to exercise his traditional authority. Jesse uses the imagery of looms and weaving to describe the glittering but pasteboard life of the Palace to which Fanny has become accustomed, and in which she appears 'a little lacquer lady come to life'. As in all great tragedies, however, the end is inevitable, and Fanny plays a part in the downfall of Upper Burma and its annexation by the British.

Jesse maintained her interest in the Far East and seventeen years later she wrote *The Story of Burma*, a concise history of the country now known as Myanmar, which she dedicated to the memory of her cousin Captain Julian Tennyson, 'killed by the Japanese when fighting to free Burma'. For much of her life she had persistent ill-health but this did not affect her passion for writing. Towards the very end she started to dictate the story of her own life but realized she would never be able to finish it. With a smile she said to a friend, 'I'm thinking of calling this life of mine *The Open Door*. Or do you think perhaps *The Half Open Door* should be enough?'

ALASTAIR GLEGG lives on Vancouver Island and has spent the last year getting used to being a great-grandfather and trying to think of rhymes for 'Covid'.

Last of the Swallows

JIM RING

It is a truth universally acknowledged that the perfect happiness of progeny is achieved only in the absence of their parents. As such circumstances are normally attended by certain obvious practical difficulties and disadvantages, they are to be found less in daily life than in fiction. In the twelve books of the *Swallows and Amazons* series, Arthur Ransome is ingenious in providing good reasons for keeping their elders and betters out of the revels of the Walker, Blackett and Callum children. In the seventh of the series he is at his most adept in placing Commander Walker in the wings but off stage until the precise moment when he is needed at the climax of the tale.

What a story it is, too! As Ransome wrote to his publisher in January 1936, 'Spirits here are rising again at last. During the last four days I have seen, grabbed, clutched and pinioned a really gorgeous idea for another book. Swallows only. No Nancy or Peggy or Captain Flint. But a GORGEOUS idea with a lovely climax inevitable and handed out on a plate.' This was the brainchild that became *We Didn't Mean to Go to Sea* (1937). Many say it is Ransome's masterpiece.

Ransome's own childhood was characterized by idyllic summers spent in the Lake District and – despite a passion for writers like Stevenson and Defoe – by his father's disappointment at his academic and athletic progress. When Cyril Ransome died in 1887, his 13-year-old son felt he had much to prove. He would make his living writing stories, stories for children.

Arthur Ransome, *We Didn't Mean to Go to Sea* (1937)
Red Fox · Pb · 352pp · £7.99 · ISBN 9780099427223

Following a precipitate marriage and the publication in 1912 of his biography of Oscar Wilde, he achieved notoriety by being sued for libel by Lord Alfred Douglas. He won the case, left his wife and fled to Russia, where he forged a reputation as a journalist with his coverage of the Bolshevik Revolution for the *Daily News* and the *Manchester Guardian*. He was familiar with the leading revolutionaries, and in 1917 he met Trotsky's personal secretary, Evgenia Petrovna Shelepina. She became his second wife. After the Armistice he based himself in the Baltic, worked as the *Guardian*'s Russian correspondent and renewed his lifelong love of sailing. His account of the building and maiden voyage of his first proper yacht appeared in 1923 as *Racundra's First Cruise* (see *SF* no. 35). With the arguable exception of *Old Peter's Russian Tales* (see *SF* no. 68), this – actually his twenty-fifth book – was the first of his works that would survive him.

By the late 1920s Ransome and his wife had settled on Lake Windermere. He was approaching the age at which his own father had died. If he were ever to escape Grub Street and fulfil his ambition to write fiction for children, now was the time. In his autobiography he calls 1930 the 'hinge year'. It saw the publication of his story of the meeting on the 'lake in the north' of the Walker and Blackett children. They call each other after their sailing dinghies. They are the Swallows: John, Susan, Titty and Roger Walker; and the Amazons: Nancy and Peggy Blackett. Memorably and famously, Commander Walker's permission for his children to camp on an island on the lake comes in the form of a telegram from his ship in Malta: BETTER DROWNED THAN DUFFERS. IF NOT DUFFERS WON'T DROWN.

Swallows and Amazons was followed in quickfire succession by *Swallowdale*, *Peter Duck* and *Winter Holiday*. The essence of these four books is that of play and make-believe. The children cast themselves as adventurers, ship-wrecked sailors, treasure-hunters and Arctic explorers, and each book is set in a graphically rendered and realistic setting, peopled by characters with whom his readers could readily identify. They are spellbinding works and they set a new standard for children's writing. Such was their popularity that in September 1935 Ransome and Evgenia were able to buy a successor to *Racundra*. The 7-ton, 34-foot cutter was renamed *Nancy Blackett* in honour of Peggy's irrepressible elder sister. A couple of difficult coastal passages in the new yacht late that autumn gave Ransome the idea for *We Didn't Mean to Go to Sea*.

The plot is simply described. The Swallows are on holiday with their mother on the East Anglian coast, awaiting the return of their father who has been serving on the China Station. He is making his way back overland via Berlin. The children befriend Jim Brading, owner of a small white cutter with the ominous name of *Goblin* (modelled, down to the last fastening, plank and halliard, on the *Nancy Blackett*). He offers to take them on a short cruise round the local rivers, the Orwell and the Stour. To this Mrs Walker agrees, subject to the solemn promise by all concerned that they do not go out to sea.

While the cutter is fog-bound in Harwich harbour, Brading goes ashore to buy petrol. Unbeknown to the Swallows, he meets with an accident that lands him in hospital. Meanwhile the *Goblin* drags her anchor and drifts out to sea. Afraid to ask for help and fearful of the shoals around the coast on which the cutter could be wrecked, the Swallows hoist sail and head out to the deeps of the North Sea. Then the wind rises, a storm threatens and breaks, and night falls. It proves impossible to turn back to safety.

Susan is aghast at breaking their promise, but John chooses to press on. When the *Goblin* reaches the far side of the North Sea, the Swallows find themselves off the coast of Holland. Taking on board a pilot, they sail into the port of Flushing only to see their father leaving on the Harwich-bound steamer. He jumps ashore, is reunited with his children, and sails them back to Harwich. On their return they are met by Brading, who fears he has lost both the children and his yacht, and by an equally distraught Mrs Walker. All are forgiven. The Commander, his wife and Brading see that the Swallows had very few choices other than those they actually made.

That the children should have sailed by themselves across the North Sea in a storm stretches the bounds of credulity, but it never breaks them because Ransome has prepared his ground carefully. That they might drift out to sea with the outgoing tide is rehearsed when they run out of petrol before the fog falls. That a vessel might be lost to the shoals or to unscrupulous salvagers is woven into an early chapter before the true action begins. John is instructed how to reef the yacht, so he knows how to do so later in the storm; the crew see where the charts are to be found; Brading's expedient of using transparent Woolworth plates as a substitute for proper navigation lights on an earlier voyage prefigures the Swallows' own such use. Commander Walker's progress across Europe is also carefully flagged so that his presence on the Harwich steamer is credible.

Inherently implausible though the tale as a whole might be, each link in the chain of events that takes them to Flushing and their meeting with their father follows as surely as autumn succeeds summer. As for the storm and the fog, and incidents like meeting a lightship and rescuing a shipwrecked kitten, in conjuring them Ransome uses all the particularity and evocative detail that had made *Racundra's First Cruise* such a success.

We Didn't Mean to Go to Sea also presents dangers far more real than those in the earlier books. There is a very real prospect of piling the *Goblin* on the sands outside Harwich. They are nearly run down by a steamer. Titty and Susan struggle desperately with seasickness. As darkness descends John very nearly falls overboard attempting to reef the cutter in the teeth of the gale. The family as a whole demonstrates a level of cohesion, courage and resourcefulness that has hitherto been no more than suggested. Here the skills – particularly of seamanship – that they have learned and honed on the lake in the north are put to the most severe of tests.

Despite a series of mischances and mistakes,

the siblings emerge from their experience unbowed; indeed, Susan overcomes her fears and seasickness to helm the *Goblin* through much of the storm. For John and Susan the North Sea crossing is a rite of passage that sees them rise to the grandest of challenges inherent in sailing: that between sailors and the mighty ocean deep. Ransome's inevitable 'lovely climax' is the reunion between father and son when the professional seaman recognizes John's achievement.

> It was the most extraordinary thing, but, though he had never said so, they all knew that for some reason or other, Daddy was rather pleased with them than otherwise. There was something in the way he looked at John.

The Commander's faith in his children has been justified. Duffers would surely have drowned.

Unless in some better place, Ransome was never reunited with his own father and never received his blessing. This he deserved, for these evergreen books explore with considerable sensitivity – among many other things – the balance between dependence and autonomy, freedom and control, discipline and indulgence, peace and conflict, presence and absence, that see-saws between parent and child. And none of them do this better than *We Didn't Mean to Go to Sea.*

JIM RING is a novelist and filmmaker, and the biographer of Erskine Childers. He is also a sailor, though notably less accomplished than Commander Walker, John Walker or indeed his own son. You can hear him discussing the beginnings of *Slightly Foxed* on our podcast, Episode 1, 'Kindred Spirits'.

Bibliography

Julia Child *et al.*, *Mastering the Art of French Cooking*   69

Shane Connaughton: the writings of   75

John Fowles, *The Magus*   54

Kenneth Grahame, *The Wind in the Willows*   7

Robert van Gulik's Judge Dee stories   65

Susie Harries, *Nikolaus Pevsner: The Life*   25

Peter Hopkirk, *The Great Game*   43

F. Tennyson Jesse: the novels of   86

Norman Lewis, *Voices of the Old Sea*   81

A. J. Liebling, *The Sweet Science*   49

Alison Lurie, *The War Between the Tates*   32

Edgar Mittelholzer, *My Bones and My Flute*   60

Walter J. C. Murray, *Copsford*   36

Eric Newby, *A Short Walk in the Hindu Kush*   18

Arthur Ransome, *We Didn't Mean to Go to Sea*   90

Flora Thompson, *Over to Candleford* & *Candleford Green*   13

Coming attractions

GALEN O'HANLON goes to the seaside · MARIANNE FISHER learns the elements of style · JONATHAN LAW enters the strange world of Trebitsch Lincoln · YSENDA MAXTONE GRAHAM reads a housewife's wartime diaries · CHRISTOPHER RUSH sees Miss Jean Brodie in her prime · SUE QUINN celebrates English cooking · ANTHONY WELLS hopes against hope

Bring history into your home with a subscription to *History Today*

SPEND TIME WITH THE PAST